At Issue

| Reality TV

Other Books in the At Issue Series:

At Issue

▌Reality TV

Ronnie D. Lankford, Book Editor

GREENHAVEN PRESS
A part of Gale, Cengage Learning

Detroit • New York • San Francisco • New Haven, Conn • Waterville, Maine • London

Christine Nasso, *Publisher*
Elizabeth Des Chenes, *Managing Editor*

© 2008 Greenhaven Press, a part of Gale, Cengage Learning.

For more information, contact:
Greenhaven Press
27500 Drake Rd.
Farmington Hills, MI 48331-3535
Or you can visit our Internet site at gale.cengage.com

For product information and technology assistance, contact us at

Gale Customer Support, 1-800-877-4253
For permission to use material from this text or product, submit all requests online at www.cengage.com/permissions

Further permissions questions can be emailed to permissionrequest@cengage.com

Articles in Greenhaven Press anthologies are often edited for length to meet page requirements. In addition, original titles of these works are changed to clearly present the main thesis and to explicitly indicate the author's opinion. Every effort is made to ensure that Greenhaven Press accurately reflects the original intent of the authors. Every effort has been made to trace the owners of copyrighted material.

Cover photograph reproduced by permission of Images.com/Corbis.

LIBRARY OF CONGRESS CATALOGING-IN-PUBLICATION DATA

Reality TV / Ronnie D. Lankford, book editor.
  p. cm. -- (At issue)
Includes bibliographical references and index.
ISBN-13: 978-0-7377-3926-8 (hardcover)
ISBN-13: 978-0-7377-3927-5 (pbk.)
1. Reality television programs--United States. 2. Reality television programs
--History and criticism. 3. Reality television programs--Social aspects. I. Lankford, Ronald D., 1962-
  PN1992.8.R43R445 2008
  791.45'6--dc22

                                                              2007050874

Printed in the United States of America
  1 2 3 4 5   13 12 11 10 09
ED050

Contents

Introduction

Reality TV has become the biggest phenomenon on American television, with ratings that surpass perennial favorites like situation comedies. More than an American phenomenon, however, reality TV now reaches audiences around the world. While critics have accused producers of exploiting contestants and pandering to viewers, they have also noted that these shows seem to engage viewers socially. Viewers often identify strongly with contestants, investing emotional energy in the ups and downs of a favorite competitor. Beyond simply watching a reality program, viewers can participate in the fate of characters, and even communicate with them via the Internet. From live video feeds to Internet chat rooms to call-in voting to text messaging to blogs, the distance between the viewer and the reality TV contestant has decreased.

From Chat Room to Text Messaging

With viewer participation, reality TV blurs the distance between the viewer and the contestant. Some viewers, in fact, literally become cast members. Others expand personal involvement by watching extended footage or by attempting to influence the outcome of a program by participating in chat rooms and blogs. Viewer involvement is further enhanced by the ability to "chat" with cast members, solidifying the feeling that the viewer really "knows" the characters of their favorite show.

Extra Film Footage and Live Feeds

Because programs seldom include all available film footage, reality TV has made extra footage available, sometimes at an added cost, online. Perhaps the most extreme example of this is *Big Brother 8*, which currently allows a 24/7 Internet feed from four video cameras (which can be watched simultaneously from the same computer monitor). Live feeds are also marketed as "uncut" and "uncensored," promising to include material not allowed on television. One advertisement reads, "Never miss a thing. Spy, watch & listen to 4 cameras at the same time." By watching the live feeds, viewers can "live" in real time with the contestants, and know about events before they air on television.

Reality TV Chat Rooms and Blogs

Reality TV chat rooms allow fans to communicate with one another and to "chat" with past and current contestants. Near the end of 2005, contestants who had been "fired" from *The Apprentice* participated in moderated chat rooms, which the *New York Times* called, "equal parts business strategy and gossip." On CBS's *Survivor* page, a "Survivors Strike Back" blog presents a panel of experts and former contestants who discuss the current season, while fans frequently create personal blogs to provide ongoing commentary about their favorite show.

Reality TV Voting

Perhaps the reality TV program best known for allowing viewers to vote is *American Idol* in the United States and *Pop Idol* in Britain. "Mass calling has become 'mass participation,'" noted the technology company Telesis, "and is now an integral part of the programme format." With *American Idol*, a separate toll-free number is assigned to each contestant, and viewers may call and cast their vote(s) within two hours of the program's airing. In the spring of 2007, National Public Radio reported that 609 million votes had been cast during the previous season. A total of 74 million votes were cast during the season's final episode, some 8 million more votes than President George W. Bush received in the 2004 election.

Other Interaction

While live feeds, chat rooms, and voting may seem to have maximized the ways in which viewers can participate in reality TV, programmers continue to push the concept. *American Idol* now allows text message voting and text message chat rooms. In the fall of 2006, the Fox Network developed the idea for a new program, *Your Instant Reality*, described as a "viewer participation program . . . that involves the audience being able to submit material, take part in challenges and vote on outcomes." Ultimately, reality TV programs like *Your Instant Reality* may blur or even eliminate the line between contestant and viewer.

Reality TV and Social Relations

Does viewer participation increase the quality of the television viewing experience? Skeptics argue no, insisting that television programmers have simply found a better way to engage, and thus retain, viewers. But even conservative commentators, who have often complained about the poor content of reality TV, have made claims of its having social value. Perhaps the biggest assertion is that viewer participation can facilitate the growth of democracy. The best recent example of this is the development of reality TV in autocratic nations. In a number of Arab countries, programs like *Super Star, Star Academy,* and *Al Wadi* allow viewers to vote, an interesting cultural phenomenon in nondemocratic nations. In China, the finale episode of *Super Girl* drew 400 million viewers and generated 8 million text message votes.

While this claim may seem extravagant, commentators are still left to ponder the social phenomenon of reality TV participation. In an age when voter turnout and civic involvement seem to be on the decline, reality TV has helped millions of people bridge cultural and political differences. And while most viewers will not consider participation on *American Idol* or *Pop Idol* as important as voting in a political contest, few citizens watch 24/7 Web footage of the campaign trail or join chat rooms of political candidates. In a sense, however, whether one views this as a positive or negative social factor seems immaterial: These programs have struck a nerve with viewers around the world, assuring their staying power for the foreseeable future. And television programmers, eager to keep ratings high, will continue to find new ways to involve viewers.

1

Reality TV Has Some Positive Attributes

Richard M. Huff

Richard M. Huff is a journalist and the author of the book Reality Television.

Reality TV has made a large impact on contemporary popular culture in a short time. It has allowed viewers to travel to new places and experience diverse cultures. Unlike many television programs, reality TV allows viewers a chance to experience the drama and emotion of real individuals in real life situations. The future direction of reality TV may be difficult to guess, but one can be sure that reality TV "is here to stay."

In the short time since reality programming has become an accepted, and embraced, form of television, it's undeniable it has had a dramatic impact on popular culture. The genre has made stars out of nobodies; given viewers a glimpse into a variety of worlds, ranging from life on a golf course (*Big Break*) to battling animal experts for a shot at hosting a show on Animal Planet (*King of the Jungle*) to life as very rich people (*Rich Girls* and *My Super Sweet 16*).

With the exception of a few prime-time dramas and comedies in the past decade, reality television has dominated the media and the office talk in recent years. No wonder, the medium has shown viewers parts of the world and people they never imagined seeing before. They've also heard things they never imagined. "I don't think I need to be rich, but I think it makes life a lot easier," Brittny Gastineau said in the first episode of E! Entertainment's *The Gastineau Girls*, about Brittny and her mother Lisa. And there were friends Ally Hilfiger (daughter of the fashion designer Tommy) and Jamie Gleicher, the teenage stars of MTV's *Rich Girls*. "We just prance around this damn city like it's, like, our shopping haven," Hilfiger said in the first episode. But she went on to add that, "Just because we're rich doesn't mean that we're not good people." Any viewer without a million bucks was immediately transported into the world of those who have money.

There have been plenty of moments like those as reality show producers use people and places to tell stories. And there have been more than enough people to populate those shows and provide moments of humor, sadness, fear, and zaniness, all in the name of entertainment. "I'm not even putting on underwear," said one of the contestants on *The Bachelor* in 2005 as she prepared for a date with Charlie O'Connell. Or there was the time on NBC's *Who Wants to Marry My Dad?*, a show where the three daughters of Marty Oakland searched through a handful of women for one good enough to marry their father. One of those contestants vying for Oakland's hand took a lie detector test in a bikini. Viewers have watched along as a group of Amish teens were introduced to mainstream life while living in Los Angeles on UPN's *Amish in the City*. And for a while FX brought the world *Todd TV*, a show in which a guy lived his life in front of the cameras, without knowing viewers at home had some input into what kinds of tasks he faced. The show failed, but it was yet another experiment along the way in the go-go years of reality television.

Reality TV Touches Our Lives

For all the silliness, and shocking moments like Verne Troyer urinating in front of the cameras on *The Surreal Life*, there are touching, even heartbreaking times, too. "My family, if I die today or tomorrow, they have nothing," boxer Najai Turpin said in an episode of Mark Burnett's *The Contender*, "But now, this gives me the opportunity to go out there and give them something. Give them something to look forward to in life." Shortly after the show ended, Turpin killed himself, making the on-air statement, which aired after the suicide, one of those touching moments reality television has been able to deliver.

The jury of viewers has already ruled that the genre is here to stay.

There have also been touching times on NBC's *Starting Over*, a show with direct roots to *The Real World*, but with a self-help twist. It's built around a group of women, each trying to fix some area of their lives, while also living together and being visited by [counselors]. There are plenty of tears, lots of smiles, and a few hugs. There have been similar moments on *Celebrity Fit Club* and *The Biggest Loser*, two weight loss shows where the end results are often positive for the players.

Sure, viewers know by now that some of the moments are manipulated or concocted by producers and tweaked in the editing bays. But that doesn't matter. What does matter is whether it's good television or not.

Reality TV Is Here to Stay

The jury of viewers has already ruled that the genre is here to stay. Just take a look at the ratings for shows such as *American Idol, Survivor,* or *Amazing Race*. Reality television is here to stay. The big question, though, is where does it go from here and what new arena can producers explore and exploit? As 2006 began, among the shows producers were seeking contestants for included a competition show on MTV for budding journalists to work at. The A&E Network was seeking couples who were spending out of control to the point it hurt their relationships. The Oxygen Network was searching for a couple to appear in a new show in which each partner's ex-lovers gave insight to the current partners. And TBS and NASH Entertainment were searching for feuding neighbors to appear in a show.

Will any of them work? That's the great unknown. Some really good ideas have failed, and others have never made it on the air. But midway through 2006, it's clear producers are willing to try just about anything, and anything touching on the human existence, such as money, sex, and shelter.

What is clear is that people talk about reality shows in ways they rarely talk about prime-time scripted entertainment. If someone does something wacky on a sitcom, it's part of the show. If someone does something equally wacky on a reality series, it's the talk of offices around the country.

Reality has captured viewers in a way that no one could have expected when CBS launched *Survivor* or even when MTV started *The Real World* in 1992. As long as it does, expect the genre to continue. It's clear producers have just touched the surface with what they can do with reality programming. Someday, if producers keep pushing, a camera will go with a guy to the moon as easily as it'll go on a date in Paris. Throw in a little alcohol, a hot tub, and attractive people, and there's no doubt the viewers will follow along.

2

Reality TV Has a Negative Influence on Society

Richard Breyer

Richard Breyer is a professor at the Newhouse School of Public Communications at Syracuse University in Syracuse, New York.

Reality TV has become omnipresent in American society, with some critics praising and others condemning the fairly recent genre. The problem with reality TV is that many viewers have become more interested in the participants of programs such as Survivor *than the people around them. The television networks, however, are nonetheless happy that viewers have identified so closely with reality TV participants: Reality TV has been very profitable. The new reality programs have their roots in* Candid Camera *and* America's Funniest Home Videos, *but there is an important difference:(Newer programs include more salacious material (sex and violence) and often promote individual ruthlessness.) But the "off-the-cuff" style of many reality TV programs, along with dramatic content, has attracted younger viewers to programs like* For Love or Money *and* Big Brother. *This success almost guarantees that the networks will continue to develop new reality programs, even though the price of reality-style programming may be reality itself.*

Does the current bumper crop of reality TV shows celebrate the improvisational abilities of the participants or their public humiliation?

Richard Breyer, "Reality TV: More Mirror Than Window," *World & I*, January 4, 2004, pp. 100–105. Copyright 2004 Washington Times Corporation, January 2004. Reproduced by permission.

Click on to any Internet search engine (*Google, Ask Jeeves*), type in the words *reality television,* and you'll find a thousand Web sites and articles about this subject. Reality television is big. It's seen by millions and discussed, critiqued, chatted about, and hyped by hundreds of thousands. Some critics are convinced that *Big Brother, Survivor,* and *Road Rules* represent a very negative trend by exposing contestants' private lives; some even see parallels with pornography. "The underlying themes are themes of humiliation and degradation. And it's part of a general trend in our culture towards making the private public," says Frank Farley, past president of the American Psychological Association. Others see the genre as an example of American democracy at its best. You can become an American idol or a survivor with your own talk show through hard work and discipline, no matter where you grew up or who you are.

My view is that there is something worrisome when viewers, especially young ones, are more involved with people they see on television than with their neighbors or families. And reality TV shows seem to draw viewers into the worlds of their casts more effectively than do sitcoms, detective shows, and other series.

From the networks' point of view, this is a good thing. In fact, for the last four summers, reality TV brought sunshine into the lives of network executives. In August 2000, CBS' *Survivor* held audiences of, on average, twenty-eight million. The next year NBC had its moment in the sun with its breakout reality show, *Fear Factor.* And in 2002 Fox won the summer sweeps with *American Idol.* [In the summer of 2003,] ABC was the winner with its popular *For Love or Money.*

Additionally, the genre has remained profitable as the weather cools. Most of CBS' highest-rated shows are in the reality TV camp—*The Amazing Race; Big Brother* series; and *Survivor* (Borneo, Australia, Africa, Marquesas, Thailand, the Amazon, twice, and the Pearl Islands). But CBS isn't alone. *Joe*

Millionaire and *American Idol* have earned big bucks and ratings for Fox; The *Real World, Road Rules,* and *The Osbournes* help pay the bills at MTV.

But as happens so often, the waters have been overfished. Notable examples of short-lived programs are Fox's *When Good Pets Go Bad, World's Scariest Police Chases,* and *World's Most Shocking Moments Caught on Tape.* Fox also got burned when the millionaire on *Who Wants to Marry a Millionaire?* was not the appealing dude initially represented on the show but turned out to be the subject of a restraining order for threatening his fiancee.

Even with these few failures, reality TV is still very popular. This shouldn't be a big surprise. Reality and television have been partners since the days when rabbit ears first appeared on the horizon. The medium was and is our window on the world. Through it we see real wars and inaugurations; we're part of real talk, real games, and real sports.

It is no longer the prank or the good fun that matters for the reality TV participant—it's the chance of winning big bucks.

However, with the exception of the quiz show descendant *Who Wants to Be a Millionaire?,* the programs that have put smiles on the faces of stockholders and network executives in the last three or four years are something new. The two closest relatives of the genre come from more innocent times: *Candid Camera,* which first appeared in 1948, and *America's Funniest Home Videos,* the still-popular series that came on the air in the early 1990s. On *Candid Camera,* audiences were there when an unsuspecting diner discovered a goldfish in her soup; on *America's Funniest Home Videos,* we witnessed Dad falling off the dock as he backed up to have his picture taken. With them, we heard the good news, "You're on *Candid Camera,*" or "You've won a thousand dollars and a chance to compete for the big money next week." These two sentences made it okay to be voyeurs and to laugh at these unfortunates because they transformed two private, mildly embarrassing moments (and many others like them) into television. When an event of any sort appears on television, it is transformed from a childish prank or a foolish mistake into something almost sacred, like the news or an episode of *Friends*. And, like the stars of *Friends* or the local news anchor, unsuspecting soup eaters and lovable dads became celebrities.

The opportunities for fame and fortune are even greater for contestants on the new reality shows. Hard to imagine the moms or sisters featured on *America's Funniest Home Videos* getting the chance that *Survivor* alumni Heidi Strubel and Jenna Morasca got. "*Playboy* made a really good offer. We felt really honored being on the cover," Morasca told *Us* magazine. Richard Hatch, the winner of the first *Survivor*, had his own radio show and all sorts of lucrative endorsement deals. It is no longer the prank or the good fun that matters for the reality TV participant—it's the chance of winning big bucks.

Another series that influenced the current crop of reality TV shows is PBS' [Public Broadcasting System's] *An American Family*, a 1973 series that took the viewer to the "every days" of the Loud family of Santa Barbara, California. We sat at their dinner table, drove with them to jobs and ballet recitals, heard their stories and, in general, watched them go about their business. Along the way we learned some of their secrets—the marriage was falling apart and one son was gay.

What made *An American Family* important was who the Louds were and where they lived. Documentaries about families and communities had been around for a long time, from Robert Flaherty's *Nanook of the North* to National Geographic specials and CBS reports. But these films were about Eskimos, life in Bombay's crowded slums, or migrant farm workers. *An American Family* was about a middle-class family, like the thousands of families who watched the series. It was not a window on the audience's world, it was a mirror.

Survivor, Road Rules, The Real World, and *Big Brother* take the foundations laid by the producers of *Candid Camera, America's Funniest Home Videos,* and *An American Family* and build something quite new. To begin with, the new reality television contains structures and story arcs that are much more complicated than backing off a dock or attending a ten-year-old's dance recital. According to Syracuse University Professor Robert Thompson, director of the Center for the Study of Popular Culture, these shows are hybrids of fiction and nonfiction. "Perhaps they most resemble jazz, another indigenous American art form in which agreed-upon rules are the jumping-off point for improvisation and the unplanned," Thompson noted in a recent National Public Radio commentary.

In CBS' summer retreat, *Big Brother 5,* the set (the *Big Brother* mansion), the cast (the "houseguests"), the games, and surprises ("X" factors) are fixed. What happens beyond these agreed-upon rules is improvised and unplanned.

Another feature of the genre is the format of the shows. Here again producers borrow from both fiction and nonfiction. In the opening minutes of the first episode of *Big Brother 5,* we meet the eight core houseguests—mostly twenty-somethings, all with movie-star good looks and figures, who are introduced with fast-paced editing that includes flashbacks of good-byes to family and jobs presented with a mix of game-show and sitcom-production techniques.

After a commercial break comes act 2 and the exposition of the plot. Here's where we learn how "guests" stay in the game, how viewers participate in the fates of the participants, and what has to be done to be the big winner who takes home five hundred grand.

In act 3, the producers of *Big Brother*—represented by a petite Asian American who speaks to the contestants though a television monitor—tell the houseguests that each has a minute to choose his or her bedroom and bed. Choices include sleeping alone or with a partner in a double bed. *Candid Camera* and *America's Funniest Home Videos* might have had mild violence (food fights, Mom backing the new Chevy into the garage door), but never a word about sex, and certainly never any action in this forbidden category. Not the case in the current reality shows, especially programs like MTV's *Spring Break*, which takes the viewers to Florida beach parties.

About twelve minutes into the first episode, after beds and partners have been selected, the group begins to bond in the mansion's spacious Diary Room. Here's where we get the first of many cutaway interviews, full face, one-on-one confessions in which a contestant fills us in on what he was really thinking when he chose his bed or partner. This is where the plot thickens because we get hints on how each contestant plans to play the game.

These now-standard confessionals make it clear that each player is out for himself, just like in the really "real" world outside the box. We are part of a culture that tells us that, while family and community are important, we are on our own in the end. According to Janelle Brown of Salon.com, this attitude is what got Richard Hatch of the first *Survivor* into the winner's circle: "Score one for good old ruthless American Capitalism, zero for the frailty of human emotions."

These interviews give control of the story to the contestants. In contrast, Allen Funt, the host of *Candid Camera*, was the star of the show who introduced each sequence, narrated events as they unfolded, and announced the magical "Smile! You're on *Candid Camera*." The anchor of *America's Funniest Home Videos* may not have as much star power as Funt, but he is in charge by providing voice-over commentary on the videos and interviewing winners.

In contrast, today's reality TV has a casual production style borrowed from MTV's *The Real World* and *The Os-*

bournes. These two series, like MTV in general, say, "We don't take television or ourselves very seriously. Let's just let the cameras roll and see what happens."

Since teens and twenty-somethings are advertisers' most sought-after demographic, it is not surprising that the MTV look has seeped into the more sophisticated, big-budget, network shows. While there is plenty of writing, editing, and producing going into *Survivor, American Idol*, and *Big Brother*, it doesn't look that way. Hosts play relatively minor roles and, it appears, the contestants "write" the show without much help from writers or producers: "The tension suddenly explodes when Scott tosses furniture around the house . . ." (*Big Brother 4*, CBS). "Jordan escorted her to the study. He offered her the chance to wager her million dollars for a second chance at love" (*For Love or Money*, ABC).

Is reality TV the crack cocaine of what critic Marie Winn calls the 'plug-in drugs?'

In addition to snagging young viewers, reality TV offers opportunities for media moguls to tie broadcast television to the Internet and find ways to make money with this new technology. "It's a never-ending show that allows for true interactive entertainment," says Adam Cohen, vice president for streaming video at Digital Island, the company that's providing video to *Big Brother 5* fans who pay $29.95 for the right to drop in at the "mansion" anytime they want, 24/7. While watching this, viewers see short streamed-video ads, timed to be "unobtrusive to the viewer," according to Cohen. The site (*Big Brother* link at CBS.com) also contains conventional banner ads, and links to the *Big Brother* store, and other sites. All these new sources of income may be the life-saving wave of the future as channel surfing, TiVo, and other new technologies deflate the value of the networks' traditional way of earning a living.

Will the reality TV fad last? Will next summer's breakthrough program be yet another *Survivor, For Love or Money,* or *Big Brother?* My guess is yes. These programs are cheap to make—at least cheaper than sitcoms and lawyer shows—and have a number of revenue streams. They're entertaining, edgy, spontaneous, and sexy. Most importantly, reality television makes it possible for the average person to be both a viewer and a TV star. Sure, I can dream about being in the cast of *Friends* or *Sex in the City,* but it's a stretch. Lose a few pounds, work on the tan, get a tattoo, and I could be the next survivor, houseguest, or road racer. The most common way to participate in a reality TV show is via the casting-call links on the various series' Web sites. There are also conventional casting calls, advertised through newspaper ads and screened by in-person auditions. And this may be why reality television continues on the screens of American viewers as well as those of network executives.

Profits and ratings aside, should we be worried that millions of viewers are choosing *The Real World* and *Road Warriors* over *West Wing, Monday Night Football,* and other types of mainstream fare? Should the FCC [Federal Communications Commission] require programs in this genre to be preceded with "The following may be hazardous to your health?" Is reality the crack cocaine of what critic Marie Winn calls the "plug-in drugs?" My answer is yes, when addicts' distorted views of reality make it impossible for them to function in the world outside the tube. Why meet the neighbors when we have the Osbournes? Why take that trip out West? *Survivor* is on at 9:00.

3

Young Viewers Are Drawn to Reality TV

Suzanne Martin

Suzanne Martin is a manager of youth and education research for Harris Interactive, a marketing research firm.

Reality TV is very popular with tweens and teens, accounting for six and a half hours of youth television viewing per week. Youth strongly identify with the participants of programs like Fear Factor, American Idol, *and* Survivor, *and are drawn to characters with a good sense of humor, physical attractiveness, and physical ability. Talking about and viewing reality TV with friends also forms an important part of many tweens'/teens' social life, though many adolescents also watch these programs alone or with family. While the total impact of the relatively new genre is difficult to measure, it is clear that reality TV has assumed a central place in tweens' and teens' television viewing habits.*

Today's youth spend many of their daily waking hours exposed to and influenced by television. According to the Kaiser Family Foundation's 2005 report, "Generation M: Media in the Lives of 8–18 Year-olds" (survey conducted by Harris Interactive), young people ages 8 to 18 spend an average of three hours per day watching TV. The influence and effects of this behavior are of perennial interest to parents, teachers, and physicians, as well as youth marketers.

Interest in the influence of television is related to both the amount of TV viewed and the content of what is watched.

Suzanne Martin, "Youth & Reality TV," *Trends & Tudes*, vol. 5, June 2006, pp. 1–4. © 2006 Harris Interactive Inc. All rights reserved. Reproduced by permission.

Tweens and teens can choose among a wide selection of programming genres. The fastest growing genre in the new millennium is reality programming. At the end of the 2003 television season, there were 29 reality series on the seven broadcast networks. Much of youth programming contains reality television programs and this genre is showing no signs of weakening. In 2002, reality programming accounted for 6.5 hours of broadcast network schedules per week and in 2004 that weekly programming jumped to 20 hours per week.

This month's issue of *Trends & Tudes* focuses on the impact of reality television in the lives of youth. Harris Interactive, in collaboration with researchers at the Center on Media and Child Health and Temple University, recently completed a survey among 1,373 teens and tweens, ages 8 to 18, in order to better explore connections between television watching, reality television, self esteem, body image and health behaviors.

Reality TV Programming that Attracts Youth

The most commonly watched reality TV shows are *Fear Factor* (69%), *American Idol* (68%), and *Survivor* (43%). Reality TV watching increases with age for most reality TV shows, with the exception of *American Idol* and *Fear Factor* which capture a large segment of tween and teen viewership.

Youth give a variety of reasons for watching their favorite reality show.

"because it shows all different countries, and teaches you their customs and their favorite foods."

—Female, 9 years old

"cause it is cool watching people eat bugs and do crazy stuff."

—Male, 11 years old

"It brings two opposites together and they both learn something about the other and the audience does too."

—Male, 16 years old

"I like the action and the excitement of seeing someone win and the disappointment of seeing someone you would like to win, get voted out or lose."

—Female, 8 years old

"Because it shows normal people going through obstacles to test how/if they can master many mind over matter obstacles. I think it is interesting to see different people's reactions to obstacles that become more difficult because of various mental blocks."

—Male, 13 years old

"It is exciting, and requires actual skill of its competitors. Shows different locations and introduces one to different cultures. It is generally clean and appropriate for me to watch with my family. The characters are often more likable to me than other reality shows."

—Female, 18 years old

"because I like to see how they pretend to be friends and then they stab them in the back. It is so life like."

—Male, 16 years old

Favorite Reality TV Characters

Tweens, and to a lesser extent, teens, identify strongly with reality TV show participants; they wish they could physically look like them (33%), dress like them (29%), be like them (24%), talk or act like them (20%), and about half (47%) even aspire to become one of them. Thirty-seven percent of tweens (ages 8 to 12) and thirty percent of teens (ages 13 to 18) feel the reality television characters are more like them than people on regular television; thus giving a potential reason behind the strong identification. About one in three (34%) believes there is a chance they could be on a reality TV program.

About half of youth don't have a favorite male (50%) or female (49%) character in reality TV shows. When youth do pick a favorite male character, the things most females prefer are his sense of humor (41%) and physical attraction (28%); while males prefer his sense of humor (40%) and athletic ability (20%). When youth pick a favorite female character, females most prefer the character's ability to get along with others (23%) and sense of humor (21%).

Social Context of Reality TV Watching

Being able to discuss popular reality TV shows is important to tweens' and teens' social status.

About half of tweens (53%) and teens (43%) like to watch reality television so they can talk to their friends about it. However, for most youth, watching reality programs is not a group activity; two-thirds of kids (66%) report that they rarely or never watch reality TV shows with their friends. Reality programs are more often watched with family—two-thirds (66%) watch reality shows with their family at least some of the time. Our survey indicates that social context during viewing is related to weight and self esteem. More youth watching reality television alone are obese, 14 percent, compared to their healthy weight peers at eight percent.

Of course, there are many types of programming that tweens and teens are watching. Do these findings regarding the influence of reality programs differ than other shows? We will leave that open to future exploration. But the current results present some interesting clues to the impact of this latest programming trend.

4

Reality TV Offers a Positive Religious Message

Margaret Feinberg

Margaret Feinberg is a writer living in Sitka, Alaska.

When Travel the Road premiered on the Trinity Broadcasting Network (TBN) in the spring of 2003, the program brought something new to the concept of reality television. First, the show was centered on two missionaries who traveled the world delivering the Christian gospel, and secondly, the show avoided gimmicks by allowing the missionaries to experience real dangers. Also unlike many reality shows, the missionaries themselves, not a network producer, developed the idea for Travel the Road, then, offered the same basic message as TBN's other programs, but provided a way for the network to reach new viewers. Reality TV, the network believes, can present a positive message.

Rather than try to land a spot on a reality television show, twentysomething Christians Tim Scott and Will Decker decided to create their own. Five continents, 25 countries, and 40,000 miles later, their adventures as missionaries play out for television audiences to see on a reality series that's actually more real than most.

Travel the Road, which premiered last spring [2003] on the Trinity Broadcasting Network (TBN), records Scott and Decker's journey from the deserts of Ethiopia to the island villages of Papua New Guinea. With only one backpack, a

Margaret Feinberg, "Reality TV on a Mission," *Christian Reader*, vol. 42, 2004, pp. 56–59. Copyright 2004 Christianity Today, Inc. Reproduced by permission of the author.

change of clothes, and a message of hope, these twentysomethings preached the gospel to anyone who would listen.

Tim Scott says the trip wasn't too different from those of
other missionaries. "We packed our Bibles and very little else
and went into the world with the willingness to preach the
gospel to those that have never heard of Jesus," he says. "The
big difference is the fact that we documented on a mini-
recorder all that the Lord was doing in our lives and all that
he is doing overseas. We documented our journey from start
to finish."

Over a period of 18 months, Scott and Decker shot more
than 300 hours of footage, "It is such a great way to open the
eyes of those that have never seen the Third World and the
mission field," Scott continues. "All it requires is a willingness
to follow the Lord."

During the first thirteen 30-minute episodes of *Travel the
Road*, viewers get to witness life as a missionary from the
mundane to the adventurous. It's *Survivor* meets *Fear Factor*
meets *The Amazing Race*, but without the rescue team standing by or a million-dollar prize at the finish line.

One of the most dangerous points of the journey, which is
captured in the latter part of the series, shows Scott and
Decker inside a tent with lions nearby. "You could hear them
sniffing, right outside," Scott recalls. "And we knew it was
common for them to maul people. It's not like it's a dog outside your tent. It's a lion! And afterward we were reading stories of safaris gone bad—anything can happen from people
being stomped by elephants to being attacked by hyenas."

Becoming Missionaries

The irony of this whole thing is that Tim Scott, 24, and Will
Decker, 28, aren't what you would consider prime candidates
for mission work. A Christian since the age of 5, Scott dreamed
of becoming a Wall Street stockbroker. A bright kid, at 16
Scott went through two years of business college and an in-

ternship at Paine Webber. He received degrees in business administration from Vision Christian Bible College in Denver where his father served as the school's president, and he planned on taking the business world by storm.

But a weeklong mission trip to the Czech Republic with his parents interrupted his dream. While abroad, Scott says he received a very specific call to the mission field. He returned to the States with a fresh resolve to preach the gospel and began to formulate a strategy through prayer.

In 1998, he headed off on his first journey and felt led to do something rather unconventional: he approached Decker, a non-Christian friend of his brother's and a professional photographer, to go with him. Scott figured Decker's photography skills could prove useful.

Ready for a change, Decker agreed to go. The twosome sold their possessions and took out loans to cover the cost of the trip. Over the next year, they visited 20 countries, and within three months of watching God move in people's lives, Decker committed his life to Christ and began preaching alongside Scott.

In 2000, the twentysomethings, whose missionary adventures have been compared to [New Testament apostles] Paul and Barnabas, headed off for a second trip, which spanned two years. But this time, they took a video camera—a Sony P100, which they knew could "take a beating"—and a third person, Scott's brother Michael, who joined them for parts of the trip.

A New Reality Show

When they returned and began viewing the footage, they knew they had something special. They approached mainstream broadcast networks, including the Discovery Channel and National Geographic Channel, about airing the series, but none were interested. Finally, the guys found a home for the show at TBN, the Christian TV network that reaches millions of viewers worldwide.

Paul Crouch, Jr., TBN's vice-president of administration, says the network was "thrilled" to land the series. It arrived at a time when TBN was looking for more compelling ways to reach the lost than just a guy standing behind a pulpit. "We want more movies and reality series, and we're really trying to push the envelope technologically," Crouch says.

Looking at the project, Crouch admits that the series probably couldn't have happened any other way than Tim and Will going out on their own the first time around. "Quite honestly, I don't know that if we would have tried to create a show like this that it ever would have happened," Crouch says. "But because they went and did it on their own, it has really worked. I think these guys have been called by God to do this, and this project was orchestrated by the Lord to get young people to go out and be a witness."

Television Missionaries

Lost in the spectacle of the reality series is the fact that Will Decker is still a fairly new Christian. His eyes light up when he talks about his recent travels. The trips, he says, place him in a position where his faith is constantly growing. "It's not like you're in the States where you have a job and a regular life," he says. "Whether you're riding on a truck across a Tibetan plateau at 18,000 feet or you're blessing a meal—you're blessing it because it really needs to be blessed, you're really out there. There are no real distractions overseas, and you're growing every day with the Lord."

In September 2003, Decker and Scott left for their third missionary trip. This one is officially backed by TBN and is estimated to last two to three years. The journey began in exotic Thailand, and will continue into Cambodia and Vietnam. But the bulk of their missionary work will take place in China, Mongolia, and Siberia.

Both Decker and Scott believe this second season will be better than the first. "It helps us having edited the first trip," Decker says. "We know what we need to say and what things people find interesting."

The new season of *Travel the Road* is scheduled to premiere [in] spring or summer [2004], which means even more viewers will get to witness Scott and Decker survive thrilling moments like crossing pirated waters, getting lost in the jungles of Laos, having stones pitched at them in Northern Ethiopia, or being covered in leeches. Scott shrugs off the hardships of their journeys as "no big deal" and just part of the fun of spreading the gospel. "There's such excitement," he says. "It's adventure with a purpose."

5

Reality TV Offers an Amoral Message

Patrick McCormick

Patrick McCormick is a professor of Christian ethics at Gonzaga University in Spokane, Washington.

Reality TV programs like Extreme Makeover *have become popular in part because they reflect Americans' obsession with beauty and youth. Many baby boomers are now choosing to have plastic surgery and Botox injections, an ironic choice for a generation that has disdained the body piercing and tattoos of their children. But the quest for youth and beauty has a dark underside, especially for the women who receive the majority of these procedures: while doctors state that these procedures are safe, they also—once upon a time—claimed that silicone implants were safe. The underlying problem with reality shows like* Extreme Makeover *is the role they play in accenting American society's fixation with surface solutions, promoting expensive procedures and eternal beauty instead of a more radical and genuine moral makeover.*

ABC-TV gave itself a major ratings facelift a few years back by asking America *Who Wants to Be a Millionaire?* Now the Disney-owned network is looking to brighten its fiscal smile with a Cinderella show that asks plain Janes and ordinary Joes "Who Wants to Be a Supermodel?" Nearly everybody, it would seem.

Patrick McCormick, "Repaint, For the Kingdom of God Is at Hand," *U.S. Catholic*, vol. 69, May 2004, pp. 44–46. Copyright © 2004 by Claretian Publications. Reproduced by permission.

When the pilot for *Extreme Makeover* came out ..., nobody expected a reality show about plastic surgery to be a big hit. But the before-and-after tale of three homely folks who go under the knife in search of beauty and happiness sucked in a fat audience of 13.2 million viewers and had network executives slicing up their spring schedule to make room for 10 new episodes. Quicker than you can get a Botox injection, ABC had a hit show, and more than 10,000 people were standing in line for a shot at free surgery.

Extreme Makeover, which tracks the six- to eight-week transformation of a couple of lucky contestants as they are run through a gamut of nose jobs, face lifts, tummy tucks, and liposuctions, appeals to both the grotesque and romantic in us. The millions of viewers who savor the graphic coverage of bodily injuries on *CSI* and *Six Feet Under* will find ample entertainment watching the insults and gore of this human chop shop. And fans of Oprah and Dr. Phil will find heartwarming encouragement and teary-eyed inspiration in these tales of insecure and unhappy folks remade in the image of beauty and success.

America's "Extreme Makeover"

The show also represents the latest (and, one hopes, last) stage in the progression of makeover programs. Years ago Martha Stewart ... made millions and then billions by showing middle-class Americans that they could set their tables and decorate their gardens like the rich and famous. This, in turn, begat shows like *Trading Spaces,* which showed ordinary folks transforming their homes into palaces. Next came *Queer Eye for the Straight Guy* and *What Not to Wear,* hit series that had the fashion police remaking folks by cleaning out closets, coiffing hair, and giving facials. Clothes (and a good haircut and manicure), it would seem, make the man or woman.

Still, these makeovers were fixing only the exteriors. TV needed a makeover show that would get under the skin, straighten teeth, fill in wrinkles, tuck tummies, suck out fat. TV audiences wanted a makeover show that would do for our bodies what others had done for our homes and closets. We wanted plastic surgery. And so *Extreme Makeover* promised to deliver the ultimate reinvention, to transform us completely by nipping and tucking away all our imperfections. As ABC Entertainment president Susan Lyne reported, this wasn't just a show about changing a person's looks, "it was actually about transforming someone's life."

Chastising youngsters who get nose rings seems a bit hypocritical if you're injecting bacteria under your eyelids every three months.

And lots of Americans seem pretty interested in the life-transforming promises of cosmetic surgery. As Baby Boomers age, millions have turned to plastic surgery and other cosmetic procedures to look younger and slimmer. [In 2003,] plastic surgeons in this country did over 8 million cosmetic procedures, nearly three times as many as [in 1998], and doctors gave more than 2 million Botox injections, nearly 40 percent more than the previous year. Americans are less inclined to hide the fact that they've had cosmetic surgery and are having procedures earlier and more often than ever before. Nearly half the people having plastic surgery or cosmetic procedures [in 2003] were between the ages of 35 and 50.

America's Obsession with Beauty

The runaway success of shows like *Extreme Makeover* and the increasing popularity of cosmetic surgery raise some interesting and perhaps uncomfortable questions. Culture critics have long been concerned with America's obsession with youth and beauty, and the narcissism of Baby Boomers is by now a familiar, perhaps even tired, complaint. Still, it seems at least a bit ironic that the very generation that so recently bemoaned their children's tendency to decorate their torsos and append-ages with body-piercing rings and colorful tattoos should be rushing in such numbers to tummy tuckers and lipo suckers. Chastising youngsters who get nose rings seems a bit hypo-critical if you're injecting bacteria under your eyelids every three months.

Maybe we need a different kind of makeover, like Fresh Veggies and Fruits for the Junk Food Guy.

Then, of course, there are the dangers, mostly to women. After almost a century of failed and failing diet fads that have resulted in eating disorders for millions, do we really want to up the ante by encouraging these women and their daughters to embrace increasingly radical and invasive surgeries and procedures so they can become—or stay—beautiful enough for their men? Among the 8.2 million cosmetic procedures conducted [in 2003], 87 percent of them were done to women. It sounds like the Stepford wives are everywhere. Meanwhile, cosmetic surgeons assure us that these procedures are increas-ingly safe. But didn't we hear those same promises about the Beverly Hills diet and silicone breast implants?

Some of the popularity of *Extreme Makeover* and cosmetic surgery must surely come from our growing despair over the war against fat. For decades Americans have consumed every diet and adopted every exercise craze that came down the pike, but we and our children continue to grow fatter. When diets and pills and flab busters have failed us, it makes sense that a lot of people would turn to the knife.

Still, maybe we need a different kind of makeover show, like *Fresh Veggies and Fruits for the Junk Food Guy*. Or maybe we could have a show where a construction crew comes into a working class neighborhood and tears down all the fast food franchises and builds food co-ops in their place. Or maybe we could have a makeover show where five bikers go into someone's garage and exchange their SUV for a 10-speed, or where bus passes become a fashion statement.

A Moral Makeover

A show about a handful of contestants winning free cosmetic surgery also raises questions about social justice in the only post-industrial country without national health care. There is something slightly obscene about a program that whets millions of people's appetites for expensive elective procedures while 40 million Americans can't afford basic health care and when the vast majority of those who are insured are not covered for these treatments. *Extreme Makeover* feels a bit like the old *Queen for a Day*, where housewives with really sad tales won new washers and dryers, except that people don't have a basic right to washers and dryers.

Jesus was into makeover. Moral theologian Charles Curran says the central message of the New Testament is Christ's call to conversion. When Jesus encountered people he called them to radically change their lives, to transform their basic ways of thinking, feeling, and acting. He told Peter and his friends to leave their nets and come follow him. He told the rich young man to give his wealth to the poor and become a disciple. He told a lame man to get up and follow him. He invited Pharisees, tax collectors, prostitutes, strangers, and fishermen to turn around and come after him. He told Nicodemus he must be born again, and he knocked Saul flat on his back and sent him off in the opposite direction.

Our consumer culture sees makeovers as a commodity, something we need to purchase on a regular basis. Every few years we need to redo our living rooms, update our wardrobe, change our hairstyle, and (now) lift our faces and smooth out our wrinkles. But the makeover Jesus wants is different. This makeover is a change of heart, a metanoia, or conversion, that reverses the very direction of our lives.

In Mark 1:14 Jesus begins his public ministry by calling people to "Repent, for the kingdom of God is at hand" and that repentance involves turning from sin to God. That's the kind of makeover no fashion police or cosmetic surgeon can do for us. But it may be the only sort of facelift that lasts.

6

Reality TV Can Change Cultural Attitudes

Ben Arnoldy

Ben Arnoldy is a staff writer for the Christian Science Monitor.

Reality TV has not only become an international affair, but has had an impact on cultural style. A TV network in Afghanistan, Tolo, has been shamed with trying to change the moral aspects of the Afghan culture by showing Reality TV and News broadcasts that conflict with conservative Afghan values with Western culture. The majority of Afghanistan is made up of those who are age 22 and under, and are ready for a change in their culture in matters of dress codes and interaction with male-female relations. Reality TV is one way that introduces Afghanistan to new Western culture and ideas, but at the same time, the country is trying to balance tradition.

A bearded man from the bazaar is whisked into a barber shop, where he's given a shave and a slick haircut. After a facial, he visits fashion boutiques.

In a few tightly edited minutes of television, the humble bricklayer is transformed into an Afghan metrosexual, complete with jeans, sweater, suede jacket, and sunglasses.

Reality TV Common in America but Risky in Afghanistan

It may sound like standard reality TV fare in the West, but it's edgy in Afghanistan. Tolo TV aired the show only once.

Ben Arnoldy, "Kabul's Must-See TV Heats Up Culture War in Afghanistan," *Christian Science Monitor*, May 10, 2005. Copyright © 2005 The Christian Science Publishing Society. All rights reserved. Reproduced by permission from *Christian Science Monitor*, (www.csmonitor.com).

But in a pop culture as barren as the mountains here, Tolo's mix of MTV-style shows and hard-hitting news programs has turned the up-and-coming network into an entertainment oasis.

Today, it's a kind of must-see TV that has government officials leaving work early to catch their favorite show. But it's also a lightning rod for Afghan critics who see the station as a threat to the country's Islamic values.

"We have to be a little bit careful, because people will start saying that we are trying to change people's culture," says Saad Mohseni, one of three Afghan brothers who started the station.

At issue is the direction of Afghanistan's next generation, those age 22 and under who make up the majority of the country.

Tolo has already drawn significant criticism for airing Indian music videos and Western films, as well as presenting shows with young hipsters who wear baseball caps sideways, talk and laugh freely with the opposite sex, and otherwise break the mold of stiff public propriety here.

Fear of Changing Values

In March, the country's *ulema shura*, or council of Islamic scholars, criticized Tolo and other stations for transmitting "programs opposed to Islam and national values." The controversy may deepen after Tolo's launch last week of satellite broadcasting, which expands its reach outside of Kabul to rural, more conservative regions.

At issue is the direction of Afghanistan's next generation, those age 22 and under who make up the majority of the country. Analysts say that the show's obvious popularity as well as the US presence here have kept the censors at bay.

"If mullahs react against Tolo, it won't matter," says Fahim Dashty, editor of the English-language Kabul Weekly. "The ministers are showing that they have more interest in a free press because they have US-backed support."

Since receiving starter funds from the US Agency for International Development and going live in October 2004, Tolo has grown into a self-sufficient operation. With a reported 81 percent share of the market, it's the most popular station in Kabul.

Youth of Afghanistan Bring Culture Change

Like Tolo, other Afghan stations broadcast a mix of news, music, and religious programming. But Tolo's style sets it apart. At the station headquarters in Kabul, almost everyone is young and dressed in tight shirts and faded jeans.

There's nary a *salwar kameez* in sight—partly because management discourages it. Young men and women work side by side without awkwardness.

This revolutionary atmosphere shows on air. The station receives plaudits for its independent, hard-hitting news programming. One recent segment of the nightly news magazine, "The 6:30 Report," tackled the issue of pedophilia, which is disturbingly common here.

The no-holds-barred news reports have been widely appreciated, even by the Taliban who have sent communications to the station to get their message out. But it's the music video hour called "Hop," and programs like "Candid Camera" knockoff "Moments" that draw the most fire for "imitating" foreigners at the expense of traditional Afghan culture.

Such broadcasts are "against our identity here, because our nation is Muslim," says Maulavi Qiam-ud-Din Kashaf, spokesman for the *ulema*.

Adjusting to New TV Broadcasting

The government has set up an independent review board to hear complaints about broadcasts, but so far the Ministry of

Information and Culture has not shut down any stations. "Banning a TV network is not the way to solve it," says Sayed Makhdoom Raheen, minister of information and culture.

'Imitation can be defined as the cleverest way of learning.'

Instead, the response by both the ministry and the *ulema* has been to put their efforts into alternative stations. The *ulema* plan to launch their own religious station with the blessing of the government.

But it's unlikely these efforts will enjoy the same popularity as Tolo, analysts say, because Tolo is tapping into issues within the youth zeitgeist.

Challenging Afghan Morals

Modesty in male-female relations and respect for elders are two important parts of Afghan culture that Tolo is challenging, Dashty and others say. They point especially to a presenter on "Hop" whose mannerisms betray a brash attitude that is "not Afghan." But if Tolo is imitating a form of Western youth culture, it doesn't bother M. Kazem Ahang, the former head of the journalism department at Kabul University.

"We are imitating science, we are imitating medicine, we are imitating journalism," he says. "Imitation can be defined as the cleverest way of learning."

"No one can say for certain what is Afghan culture," says Jahid Mohseni, another Tolo director. "There are a lot of vocal comments about why this is not Afghan. But the reality is people are watching it." Interviews with young Afghans here reveal similar divisions.

"We will progress and adapt ourselves according to our own culture," says 26-year-old medical student Massoud Nasimi. "The way of progress is step by step."

Other educated young Kabulis express similar sentiments. But some younger and less-educated residents feel differently.

"I don't think it's right to say that the way people wear clothes will affect their religion or culture," says Shahab Temori, a 19-year-old dressed in a jeans and a Harley Davidson belt buckle. "We will not forget our *salwar kameez*, our Afghan culture. But we will also wear these new things, too."

7

Reality TV Relies on Questionable Ethical Practices

Douglas McCollam

Douglas McCollam is a contributing editor for the Columbia Journalism Review.

Reality TV sometimes relies on questionable ethical practices, even when—on the surface—it purports to be serving a social purpose. One such program is Dateline NBC's To Catch a Predator. *While most viewers will deem the general purpose of the program—to catch sexual predators over the Internet—socially responsible, the program's methods sometimes seem geared more toward creating controversy, fear, and drama than solving social problems. In one instance, an arrest of a suspect was conducted in a nonroutine fashion, possibly to capture the drama of the moment. But before the suspect could be arrested, he committed suicide. At times,* To Catch a Predator *also seems to be working closely with the police, causing possible conflicts of interest; at other times, the individuals who pose as underage girls ask leading questions. In the end,* To Catch a Predator *evokes an atmosphere that frightens parents and adults about children's safety, when most sexual abuse is initiated by family members and family friends.*

It was just before 3 p.m. on a Sunday afternoon [in November 2006] when a contingent of police gathered outside the home of Louis Conradt Jr., a longtime county prosecutor liv-

Douglas McCollam, "The Shame Game," *Columbia Journalism Review*, vol. 45, January–February 2007, pp. 28–33. © 2007 Columbia University, Graduate School of Journalism. Reproduced by permission of the publisher and the author.

ing in the small community of Terrell, Texas, just east of Dallas. Though the fifty-six-year-old Conradt was a colleague of some of the officers, they hadn't come to discuss a case or for a backyard barbeque. Rather, the veteran district attorney, who had prosecuted hundreds of felonies during more than two decades in law enforcement, was himself the target of an unusual criminal probe. For weeks the police in the nearby town of Murphy had been working with the online watchdog group Perverted Justice and producers from *Dateline NBC's* popular *To Catch a Predator* series in an elaborate sting operation targeting adults cruising the Internet to solicit sex from minors. *Dateline* had leased a house in an upscale subdivision, outfitted it with multiple hidden cameras, and hired actors to impersonate minors to help lure suspects into the trap. As with several similar operations previously conducted by *Dateline*, there was no shortage of men looking to score with underage boys and girls. In all, twenty-four men were caught in the Murphy sting, including a retired doctor, a traveling businessman, a school teacher, and a Navy veteran.

Conradt had never shown up at the *Dateline* house, but according to the police, using the screen name "inxs00," he did engage in explicit sexual exchanges in an Internet chat room with someone he believed to be a thirteen-year-old boy (but was actually a volunteer for Perverted Justice). Under a Texas law adopted in 2005 to combat Internet predators, it is a second-degree felony to have such communications with someone under the age of fourteen, even if no actual sexual contact takes place. Armed with a search warrant—and with a *Dateline* camera crew on the scene—the police went to Conradt's home to arrest him. When the prosecutor failed to answer the door or answer phone calls, police forced their way into the house. Inside they encountered the prosecutor in a hallway holding a semiautomatic handgun. "I'm not going to hurt anybody," Conradt reportedly told the police. Then he fired a single bullet into his own head.

Standing outside the house with his crew, the *Dateline* correspondent Chris Hansen said he did not hear the shot that ended Conradt's life, but did see his body wheeled out on a gurney. Discussing Conradt's death over lunch a couple of weeks later, I asked Hansen how it made him feel. Hansen said his first reaction was as a newsman who had to cover the story for his network (Hansen filed a report the next morning for NBC's *Today* show). Hansen said that on a human level Conradt's death was a tragedy that, naturally, he felt bad about. But he understood the true import of my question: "If you're asking do I feel responsible, no," Hansen said. "I sleep well at night."

Reality TV Justice

Others aren't so sanguine. Galen Ray Sumrow, the criminal district attorney of Rockwall County, Texas, who heads the office where Conradt worked as an assistant district attorney, has reviewed evidence surrounding the case and believes it was badly botched. Among the problems he cites are that the search warrant obtained by the Murphy police officers was defective because it had the wrong date and listed the wrong county for service, basic errors that he believes would have gotten any evidence seized from Conradt's home tossed out of court. He is also mystified as to why the police would force their way into Conradt's home when they could have tried to talk him out, or just picked him up at work the next day. "He was here in the office every morning," says Sumrow, who is himself a former police officer and has been prosecuting cases for more than twenty years. "You generally like to do an arrest like that away from the home to avoid things like what happened." A sworn affidavit supporting the warrant also shows that the information about Conradt's online activities was given to the Murphy police by Perverted Justice just hours before they went to arrest him. Why were the police in such a rush to pick up Conradt? Texas Rangers are investigating that question, but Sumrow thinks he knows the answer: "It's reality television," he says. Sumrow says an investigator told him the police pushed things because the *Dateline* people had plane tickets to fly home that afternoon and wanted to get the bust on film for the show. He says investigators also told him that film excerpts show *Dateline* personnel, including Hansen, interacting with police on the scene, supplying them with information, and advising them on tactics. Sergeant Snow Robertson of the Murphy police says accommodating *Dateline's* schedule "wasn't a factor at all." Rather, he says, the urgency was to keep Conradt from contacting another minor. *Dateline's* Hansen confirms that he was to fly out that Sunday, but says such plans are always subject to change and that he hadn't even checked out of his hotel. He also denies advising the police during the operation at Conradt's house. "This stuff is not remotely based in fact," Hansen says.

The notion of delighting in another's disgrace drives much of the reality TV phenomenon.

At a town meeting called to discuss the *Dateline* sting operations, several Murphy residents expressed outrage that a parade of suspected sexual predators were lured to their community. Neighbors recounted police takedowns and car chases on their blocks, and some said fleeing suspects tossed drugs and other contraband into their yards. In a statement to the Murphy City Council, Conradt's sister, Patricia, directly implicated *Dateline* in her brother's death. "I will never consider my brother's death a suicide," she said. "It was an act precipitated by the rush to grab headlines where there was no evidence that there was any emergency other than to line the pockets of an out-of-control group and a TV show pressed for ratings and a deadline." She added: "When these people came after him for a news show, it ended his life." In an interview, she was even more direct: "They have blood on their hands," she said, referring to *Dateline*, the police, and Perverted Justice.

In a sense, Conradt's death was a tragedy foretold. In a piece for *Radar* magazine about the show, the writer, John Cook, quoted an unnamed *Dateline* producer as saying that "one of these guys is going to go home and shoot himself in the head." When I asked Hansen and David Corvo, *Dateline's* executive producer, if they were reviewing the show's procedures in light of Conradt's death, both said that there was no evidence to suggest that Conradt was aware of *Dateline's* presence when he shot himself (though a camera crew was apparently on his block for hours before the police arrived), and that there were no plans to alter how the *Predator* series is handled. "I still feel like the show is a public service," said Corvo. "We do investigations that expose people doing things not good for them. You can't predict the unintended consequences of that. You have to let the chips fall where they may."

Predator's Successful Formula

The reluctance to tinker with the show's formula is no doubt attributable to the fact that since its debut in the fall of 2004, *To Catch a Predator* has been the rarest of rare birds in the television news world: a clear ratings winner. The show regularly outdraws NBC's other primetime fare. It succeeds by tapping into something that has been part of American culture since the Puritans stuck offenders in the stockade: public humiliation. The notion of delighting in another's disgrace drives much of the reality TV phenomenon, and is present in the DNA of everything from *Judge Judy* to *Jackass* to *Borat*. *Predator* couples this with a hyped-up fear of Internet sex fiends, creating a can't-miss formula. The show's ratings success has made it a sweeps-week staple and turned Chris Hansen into something of a pop-culture icon. To date, by the show's own count, it has netted 238 would-be predators, thirty-six of whom have either pleaded guilty or been convicted. Hansen regularly gives talks to schools and parent groups concerned about Internet sex predators, and he was even summoned to Washington to testify before a congressional subcommittee investigating the problem, where he and *Dateline* received effusive praise for their efforts. When the comedian Conan O'Brien filmed a bit to open [the 2006] Emmy Awards that showed him parading through the sets of hit shows of every network, his last stop was a *Predator* house where Hansen confronted him and O'Brien gave a spot-on rendition of the sweaty, shaky dissembling that most of the show's targets display.

All that is a long way from where *To Catch a Predator* started. The *Dateline* producer Lynn Keller says she first contacted the Perverted Justice group about the possibility of doing a show in January or February of 2004. Perverted Justice had already worked with several local television stations, including one in Detroit, where Chris Hansen knew one of the producers and had talked with him about a sting operation the station had filmed using Perverted Justice's online expertise to lure targets. *Dateline*'s first sting house was set up in Bethpage, Long Island, about an hour outside of New York City. Hansen recalls being nervous that no one would show up and that he might have to explain to the network why he had blown a bunch of money on a flop investigation. "We thought we might get one person," Keller recalls. They needn't have worried. Before he could even reach the house for the first day of filming, Hansen got a frantic call from Keller that the first target was inbound. Hansen beat him there by just fifteen minutes.

The show has an undeniable "ick" factor.

The Long Island sting netted eighteen suspects in two and a half days. Eight months later, the show set up a sting house in Fairfax, Virginia (at a home belonging to a friend of Hansen's in the FBI), and snared nineteen more men, including a rabbi, an emergency-room doctor, a special-education teacher, and an unemployed man claiming to be a teacher, who memorably walked into the house naked. The third show, filmed in early 2006 in southern California, drew fifty-one men over three days. But even as the stings expanded and ratings soared, critics inside and outside the network raised serious questions about whether *To Catch a Predator* was erasing lines that even an increasingly tabloid newsmagazine show should respect.

To begin with, the show has an undeniable "ick" factor. The men (and to date they are all men) are mostly losers who show up packing booze and condoms. It is also undeniably compelling television. Each show follows a similar pattern: after asking the mark to come in, the decoy disappears to change clothes or go to the bathroom. Then, in a startling switcheroo, Hansen appears from off-stage and directs the man to take a seat. The men almost always comply, concluding that Hansen is either a cop or a father. The marks then proffer comical denials about what they are doing at the house, which never include their intent to have sex with a minor. Hansen then produces some particularly salacious details from their Internet chat with the decoy ("But you said you couldn't wait to pour chocolate syrup all over her and lick it off with your tongue"). The mark then switches gears to say he has never done anything like this before and was just kidding around or role playing, which in turn cues Hansen to say something like, "Well, you're playing on a big stage, because I'm Chris Hansen from *Dateline NBC*," at which point cameras enter from off stage like furies summoned from hell. The mark, now fully perceiving his ruin, usually excuses himself, often pausing to shake hands with Hansen—the cult of celebrity apparently transcends even this awful reality—then exits into the waiting arms of police outside who swarm him as if he had just shot the president.

Conflicts of Interest

The police busts are the emotional capper to the encounter, one that highlights the show's uncomfortably close affiliation with law enforcement. On the first two *Predator* stings, the show didn't involve arrests, an omission that garnered complaints from viewers and cops alike. Though certain individuals from the initial episodes were subsequently prosecuted, the lack of police involvement from the outset made it hard to make cases that would stick. "The number one complaint from viewers was that we let them walk out," says Keller. Starting with the third show and in the five subsequent stings, police were waiting to take down the suspects. In our interview and in his congressional testimony, Hansen is careful to refer to those arrests as "parallel" police investigations, as if they just happened to be running down the same track as *Dateline*, but the close cooperation is always evident. At a time when reporters are struggling to keep law enforcement from encroaching on newsgathering, *Dateline*, which is part of NBC's news division, is inviting them in the front door—literally. Hansen tried to deflect this criticism of the show by saying that the volunteers from Perverted Justice serve as a "Chinese wall" between the news people at *Dateline* and the police.

But as we've learned from recent corporate scandals, such Chinese walls are often made of pretty thin tissue. In the case of *To Catch a Predator*, Perverted Justice does most of the groundwork preparing the shows and roping in the men. Initially, *Dateline*'s responsibility was to cover the group's expenses, procure the house and outfit it with hidden cameras and, of course, supply Chris Hansen and airtime. However, after the third successful *Predator* show, Perverted Justice hired an agent and auctioned its services to several networks. NBC ended up retaining the group for a fee reported in *The Washington Post* and elsewhere to be between $100,000 and $150,000. Hansen would not confirm an amount but said he saw nothing wrong with compensating the group for its services, likening it to the way the news division will sometimes keep a retired general or FBI agent on retainer. "In the end I get paid, the producers get paid, the camera guy, why shouldn't they?" says Hansen.

On the surface that certainly seems reasonable, but it ignores a few relevant points. First, Perverted Justice is a participant in the story, the kind of outfit that would traditionally be covered, not be on the news outlet's payroll. "It's an advocacy group intensely involved in this story," says Robert Steele, who teaches journalism ethics at the Poynter Institute. "That's different from hiring a retired general who is no longer involved in a policy-making role." Second, it is clearly a no-no, even at this late date in the devolution of TV news, to directly pay government officials or police officers. Yet in effect that's what *Dateline* did in at least one of its stings. The police in Darke County, Ohio, where *Dateline* set up its fourth sting in April 2006, insisted that personnel from Perverted Justice be deputized for the operation so as not to compromise the criminal cases it wished to bring against the targets. After some discussion, NBC's lawyers agreed to the arrangement, which the network shrugs off as less than ideal but an isolated circumstance.

The image projected by the Predator *series is clearly meant to inflame parental fears about violent Internet sex fiends.*

Further, though Hansen and *Dateline* reject allegations that they are engaging in paycheck journalism by paying Perverted Justice—arguing for a distinction between paying a consultant and paying a source for information—the line looks a little fuzzy. For example, Xavier von Erck, who founded Perverted Justice, says via e-mail that the operation had come to a point where it could "not bear any further costs relating to the shows. Hence, we obtained a consulting fee." In turn, local law enforcement groups have stated that without the resources provided by Perverted Justice they couldn't afford to do the criminal investigations they've mounted in conjunction with the *To Catch a Predator* series. See the problem? But for NBC's deep pockets, no "parallel" police actions would take place. And are they really parallel? One lawyer I spoke with, who asked not be identified because her client's case is still pending, claims the man was entrapped and said she has every intention of subpoenaing members of *Dateline's* staff to testify if the case goes to trial. "They are acting as an arm of law enforcement and are material witnesses," the lawyer said. "They definitely crossed a line."

Entrapment and Leading Questions

There is also the question of whether the series is fair to its targets. Let's concede up front that this is an unsympathetic bunch of would-be perverts. But are they really that dangerous? Hansen himself divides those snared in the probes into three groups: dangerous predators, Internet pornography addicts, and sexual opportunists. But by Hansen's own calculation fewer than one in ten of the men who show up at a sting house have a previous criminal record.

But the image projected by the *Predator* series is clearly meant to inflame parental fears about violent Internet sex fiends. The show has invoked the specter of famous child abduction cases like [that of] Polly Klaas. The very term "predator" calls to mind the image of the drooling, trench-coated sex fiend hanging out at the local playground with a bag full of candy. Reading through the chat transcripts posted on the Perverted Justice Web site, however, it seems clear that a lot of the men snared aren't hard-core predators. Many express doubts about what they're doing and have to be egged along a bit by the decoys, many of whom come off as anything but innocent children. Consider a few of these exchanges. In the first, the mark (johnchess2000) is talking to someone he believes is an underage girl (AJ's Girl). She has agreed to let him come over to watch a movie:

johnchess2000: anything you want me to wear or bring?

AJ's Girl: hmm

johnchess2000: wow your thinking for a long time

AJ's Girl: lol sowwy

AJ's Girl: u beter bring condoms

johnchess2000: wow. condoms???

johnchess2000: wow. your thinking big huh?;0

johnchess2000:;)

AJ's Girl::"

johnchess2000: wow so you like me that much?:)

AJ's Girl: maybe

johnchess2000: maybe?? why did you say condoms?

AJ's Girl::" i duno

johnchess2000: haha. be honest

johnchess2000: you must like me a lot then huh?

AJ's Girl: yea

AJ's Girl: ur cute

Or this exchange between Jason, a twenty-one-year-old fireman and the decoy, a girl he thinks is thirteen:

jteno72960: so what kinda guys u like

katiedidsings: hot fireman 1s

jteno72960: ok what else is sexy to you

katiedidsings: tats

jteno72960: i have 2 inside my arm

jteno72960: will u kiss them for me?

katiedidsings: ya

jteno72960: what about on the lips

katiedidsings: ya

jteno72960: i love to kiss

katiedidsings: me 2

jteno72960: really what else

katiedidsings: i dunno watevr u wantd 2 do

jteno72960: well what have u done

katiedidsings: evry thing

katiedidsings: wel not evrything

katiedidsings: but alot of stuff

jteno72960: well what did u like

katiedidsings: from behind

Or this last exchange between Rob (rkline05) a twenty-year-old from Ohio, and *Dateline*'s online decoy "Shia," who poses as an underage girl. After days of chatting, Rob expresses doubts about their age difference and about a sexual encounter, but Shia dismisses his concerns and reassures him:

rkline05: but idk about everything we talked about

shyshiagirl: why not

rkline05: well you sure you wana do all that

shyshiagirl: yeaa why not

rkline05: idk i just wasnt sure you wanted to you are a virgin and all

rkline05: you sure you want it to be me that takes that

shyshiagirl: yea why not. ur cool

rkline05: i just . . . you really sure i feel weird about it you being so much younger than me and all

shyshiagirl: ur not old. dont feel weird

Rob came to the *Dateline* sting house and later pleaded guilty for soliciting a minor online.

Entrapment is a legal term best applicable to law enforcement. Perverted Justice says it's careful not to initiate contact with marks, nor steer them into explicit sexual banter. But as these chats and others make clear, they are prepared to flirt, literally, with that line. Under most state statutes passed to combat online predators, the demonstrated intent to solicit sexual acts from a minor is sufficient to land you in jail regardless of whether the minor is a willing participant. So, as a legal matter, the enticements offered by the decoys are of little importance to the police, or to issue advocates like Perverted

Justice. But journalistically it looks a lot like crossing the line from reporting the news to creating the news.

Dateline has run afoul of this distinction before. Famously, in 1993, several producers and correspondents were fired for rigging a General Motors truck to explode in a crash test. More recently the program took heat for bringing Muslim-looking men to a NASCAR race to see what might happen (the program never aired). *Predator* seems to fall somewhere between those two examples. Perhaps its most direct counterpart in recent journalistic history is the famous sting operation mounted by the *Chicago Sun Times*. In 1978 the paper set up the Mirage Tavern in Chicago and snared a host of city officials for seeking bribes from the "owners," who were actually undercover reporters. The Mirage was controversial in its day, but it seems tame by comparison to the *Dateline* stings. Al Tompkins, who teaches the ethics of television journalism at the Poynter Institute, draws a clear distinction between the Mirage and *Predator*. Mirage, he notes, was targeted at public officials who were known to be abusing the power of their offices for personal enrichment. "It was a legit question whether you could have covered the story any other way," Tompkins says. "You couldn't go through law enforcement because you didn't know if police were involved in the corruption." Tompkins, who has watched the *Dateline* series, says it looks more like a police prostitution sting than a news investigation.

Public Good or Disservice?

Dateline has argued that *Predator* serves a genuine public good, but it could be argued that, in fact, *Dateline* is doing the public a disservice. When [U.S.] Attorney General Alberto Gonzales gave a speech about a major initiative to combat the "growing problem" of Internet predators, he cited a statistic that 50,000 such would-be pedophiles were prowling the Net at any given moment and attributed it to *Dateline*. Jason McLure, a reporter at *Legal Times* in Washington, D.C., (where

I was formerly an editor), asked the show about the number. *Dateline* told him that it had gotten it from a retired FBI agent who consulted with the show. When the agent was contacted he wasn't sure where the number had come from, terming it a "Goldilocks" figure—"Not small and not large." He added that it was the same figure that was used by the media to describe the number of people killed annually by Satanic cults in the 1980s, and before that was cited as the number of children abducted by strangers each year in the 1970s. *Dateline* has now disowned the number, saying solid statistics about Internet predators are hard to find, but that the problem seems to be getting worse, a sentiment echoed by lawmakers in Congress.

But actually there isn't much evidence that it is getting worse. For example, many news reports have cited a Justice Department study as saying that one in five children is approached online by a sexual predator. But as Radford Benjamin of *The Skeptical Inquirer* pointed out, what that 2001 study actually said was that 19 percent had received a "sexual solicitation" online, about half of which came from other teens and none of which led to a sexual assault. According to the study, the number of teens aggressively solicited by adults online was about 3 percent. A more recent study by the Crimes Against Children Research Center at the University of New Hampshire found that the number of kids getting unwanted sexual advances on the Internet was in fact declining. In general, according to data compiled by the National Center for Missing and Exploited Children, more than 70 percent of sexual abuse of children is perpetrated by family members or family friends.

That doesn't mean Internet sex predators don't exist, but *Dateline* heavily skews reality by devoting hour after hour of primetime programming to the phenomenon. As Poynter's Tompkins notes: "Is there any other issue that's received that much airtime? The question is whether the level of coverage is proportional to the actual problem."

The answer, it seems, is no, and the explanation of why *Dateline* has seized on this mythical trend to anchor its venerable news show is that reality TV has so altered the broadcast landscape that traditional newsmagazine fare—no matter how provocative—just doesn't cut it anymore. "Reality programs came in and newsmagazines no longer looked so great," says one former producer for NBC News. While newsmagazines are cheap compared to other primetime shows, they don't have the potential to be gigantic hits like *Survivor* or *American Idol*. For that reason, the producer notes, the entertainment divisions at the networks never really liked newsmagazines, which they had little hand in producing and for which they received no credit. At NBC, the former producer says, Jeff Zucker, formerly the president of the network's news and entertainment group and now the c.e.o. of its television operations, regularly put the squeeze on *Dateline*, maintaining that the network needed its time slots to either develop new programming or schedule hit shows. "About the only thing they really want newsmagazines to do now is crime," says the former producer. "If it's not crime, they don't think they can sell it. The traditional investigative reporting on shows like *Dateline*, or *48 Hours*, or *Primetime Live* is no more." (A notable exception, he says, is *60 Minutes*.)

Dateline's executive producer David Corvo prefers to see the change as a setting aside of older journalistic conventions to focus on new kinds of issues. The *Predator* series, he says, is just another form of enterprise journalism, one suited to the Internet age. But the distinction between enterprise and entertainment can be a difficult one. *Dateline* hasn't so much covered a story as created one. In the process it has further compromised the barrier between reporters and cops that is central to the mission of journalism. If humiliating perverts and needlessly terrifying parents is the best use that newsmagazines can make of hours of primetime television, then perhaps they should be allowed to die and the time given over to the blood sport of reality programming. At least no one would dare to call it news.

8

Reality TV Can Overcome Questionable Ethical Practices

Derek Draper

Derek Draper is a British psychotherapist whose writings have appeared in the Guardian, New Statesman, *and other UK publications.*

Many people believe that reality TV is unsuited for serious pursuits such as psychotherapy and that TV would only turn such therapy into vulgar theater. The results of one such experiment on Kyle's Academy, *however, demonstrate quite the opposite. While reality TV therapy may have limitations, several subjects on this program benefited from it. People who object to TV therapy also express a form of elitism: Of the many people who suffer from psychological problems, few receive professional help. The therapy conducted on* Kyle's Academy *was conducted by a trained professional on real people and may be potentially helpful to anyone watching the program.*

I had expected a bad reaction, but was still taken aback by the sheer ferocity. "You just can't do it," my friend spluttered. "It's terrible to get people to talk about that kind of thing in public. Terribly damaging." He was appalled. "You absolutely mustn't do it."

He had just heard that I had been asked to take part in a new ITV1 show which would televise real-life therapy. Jeremy Kyle, a notoriously confrontational daytime talk-show presenter, was leaving his hothouse studio for two weeks and

moving into a made-for-TV residential treatment centre—
Kyle's Academy—to oversee five troubled volunteers undergo
therapeutic treatment. My role was to be their resident psycho-
therapist, providing intensive individual therapy—all on camera. And, to be honest, I was not sure it was a good idea myself.

My friend's horror summed up a view I encountered everywhere. TV therapy, I was told, smacked of "vulgarity", "ex-
ploitation" and "sheer bloody tackiness". These misgivings
have made no dent in the public's appetite for emotionally
raw media, though, as evidenced by the booming sales of
"misery memoirs" and magazines peddling personal trauma
tales, and in the explosion of psychological TV. Talkshow veteran Trisha has recently launched Five's *Families at War*; viewers can go into BBC3's Panic Room, or visit Channel 4's *Houses
of Obsessive Compulsives and Agoraphobics*. They can take their
children to Tanya Byron's BBC3 *House of Tiny Tearaways*—or
call in *Supernanny*.

But *Kyle's Academy* will be the first British television show
to broadcast genuine therapy sessions between a patient and a
psycho-therapist. The five participants selected to stay in the
Surrey mansion suffered from depression, obsessive compul-
sive disorder (OCD), anxiety, panic attacks, rage and guilt.
They received treatment from a nutritionist, an exercise expert
and coaches Gill Harvey-Bush and Annie Ashdown, as well as
from myself, both as a group, and individually—with some
remarkable results. Viewers can watch their emotional journeys unfold every day for the next two weeks, and get an un-
precedented glimpse into the secret world of a psycho-
therapist's consulting room.

I always knew it would make gripping television, but that
was never the issue. This kind of "emotional reality TV" raises
fundamental ethical concerns—the first being, does it work
for the participants? None of us knew whether we would
change five people's lives for ever, or leave them feeling as if

their problems had just been aired for entertainment. Even more importantly, what about the viewers? Could a TV show teach insights that they could all apply usefully to their own lives, and therefore popularise therapy among people it might never otherwise reach? Or is it just intrinsically unedifying—even coarsening? And if so, were we in danger of damaging the image of the whole therapeutic profession?

Reality TV and Therapy

Kyle's name alone will be enough to put plenty of people off. He is that rare figure who can unite the *Guardian* and the *Daily Mail*; *Guardian* columnist Charlie Brooker compared him to Satan, while the *Mail* called him a "barking ringmaster". The *News of the World* attacked him for letting a paedophile appear on his show. It is fair to say that Kyle does not get good press. But once you get past the media caricature, he is often surprisingly sensitive. His persona is that of a supportive but firm father-figure—something the guests on his show have almost always lacked in their lives, and often respond to. He is none the less a showman, representing all the perplexity, impatience and downright anger he instinctively knows will be stirred up in his viewers by what they see on screen.

My job was to recreate, as far as we were able, a genuine therapy session.

Because of my old incarnation as a New Labour spin doctor, I have been offered a lot of psychology TV work since I retrained as a psychotherapist. But the programme proposals always reek of desperation, relying on contrived confrontation and inbuilt sensationalism to reel in apathetic viewers. A show about eating disorders that I turned down, for example, emerged billed as *Freaky Eaters*—and that was on BBC. Not quite the right therapeutic tone. I also turned down the chance to be involved in the latest *Big Brother*. But Kyle's involvement actually guaranteed that the show would be less sensational than it might otherwise have been. ITV executives know his appearance acts as an insurance against anything too abstract, and so they were willing to allow a fairly unflashy format for the show.

My job was to recreate, as far as we were able, a genuine therapy session. I was not sure it was possible. Nothing I have ever done has been harder work, or made me more nervous. In this age of confession and instant celebrity, I was worried that the participants might exaggerate or grandstand. I would be a liar if I said I had no worries about my own narcissistic tendencies. But I hope I avoided playing up to the camera— and the five volunteers definitely did, remaining calmly anchored in the issues that had brought them there. As soon as we sat down face-to-face for a session, it seemed uncannily like real therapy, and that comes across on screen.

I used a mixture of cognitive behavioural therapy (CBT), to give them specific tools and techniques, coupled with deeper emotional work—what I call CBT Plus. . . . Each client had five sessions with me, and these were filmed without interruption—although during one, where the client talked of crying himself to sleep every night as a kid, the sound man had to adjust his levels to cover up his own quiet sobs. Even Kyle was moved, far more deeply, I suspect, than he had expected to be.

Treating a lucky few on TV will never make a difference to . . . national statistics, of course.

Real Help for Real Problems

So did it help the volunteers? Critics will argue, naturally, that people shouldn't have to go on TV to get help. Indeed, one of the volunteers was quite blunt: "If I could have found therapy outside, I wouldn't be here." She is right, but of the one in six of us suffering from an emotional disorder, fewer than one in 80 will get the treatment we need, according to a recent York University study. Imagine if that were true of cancer, strokes or road accident victims. It would be unthinkable.

Of the five people we treated on the show, four made solid, if understandably incomplete, progress, and I offered each some follow-up sessions. Ex-soldier Andy started sleeping, and got rid of a lot of his guilt and grief. Single parent Donna opened up about her mother's sudden death, and conquered her panic and phobia of medicine. Tracey became more intimate with her father, and started getting anger under control. Craig lessened the grip of his OCD, and his self-esteem visibly soared. For me, the progress they made was remarkable, and settled any doubts about the efficacy of televised treatment.

Treating a lucky few on TV will never make a difference to those national statistics, of course. If participants are the only ones to benefit, you would have to ask whether it was worth it. But Kyle can command a million viewers, and thousands could learn from what they see. As well as offering specific help for problems such as sleep and anger management, the early episodes validate men crying, educate viewers about grief, and demonstrate that emotions are better expressed than repressed. They also destigmatise the basic idea of therapy—a more radical achievement than you might imagine. I know of one well-heeled private patient, for example, who tells their nearest and dearest that their therapist is a reflexologist, and another whose family thinks they are seeing a French language tutor.

So did my panicky friend have nothing to worry about? Well, not quite. The fifth volunteer, Sara, is not sure she benefited much, and anyone watching will see that she makes less progress than the others. For some, this partial failure may be enough to condemn the whole programme. Yet Sara has taken up the offer of my follow-up sessions. And, as any therapist will tell you, therapy will fail with certain patients. Some patients can be disappointed and end up hating the therapy, even the therapist. It neither makes nor destroys the case for therapy; it is just one person's experience.

Therapy for Television Viewers

The greatest criticism of this kind of programme comes from therapists themselves. Even the respected clinical psychologist Tanya Byron, who also presents BBC3's *Little Angels*, has said, "Sometimes this sort of TV exploits rather than helps," and I know of one therapist who was cross-examined by his professional body, simply for giving advice on a Radio 2 phone-in. To those who consider confidentiality the sine qua non of therapy, the risk that a client might say something on camera that they would regret will always outweigh any possible benefits.

I suspect the cameras played a big part in Sara's lack of progress—for we identified early on that she wore a mask to get through life, and I fear she felt too exposed to reveal much of her "real" self on the show, though she had begun to in our sessions. But despite the difficulties, I think it was worthwhile. And let's not be too elitist about this; the alternative to *Kyle's Academy* on telly, after all, is not Oliver James but Jerry Springer. It would be great to prove that viewers will gravitate towards emotional reality shows that leave them feeling good instead of grubby.

I often tell my patients that there is a little bit of every mental illness in all of us: depression, panic, narcissism, even psychosis. There is also a bit of the exhibitionist and voyeur. In my view, it is much better to accept these parts of us, and put them to good use, whether we are one of the few on the TV studio couch, or the millions on the sofa at home just watching.

9

Reality TV Lacks Diversity

Judith Halberstam

Judith Halberstam is a professor of English at the University of Southern California and author of Female Masculinity.

Reality TV likes formulas, and one of its favorite formulas centers on relationships and marriage; for example, The Bachelor. *Reality marriage programs, in fact, have replaced sitcoms about marital relationships, such as* Roseanne, *as well as about single life, like* Friends. *But instead of supporting the idea of romance, many of these shows reveal the surface tendencies of the contestants: most contestants would rather have the good-looking or wealthy male-female companion than the compatible one. Many contestants also use the program as a launching pad for a modeling or acting career. Worse still, these programs offer only limited diversity, often bypassing persons of color and women of differing gender identification. In the end, the dramatic content of reality TV programs that center on marriage has more to say about the needs of reality TV than about matrimony.*

Marriage. Is it: (1) an intimate union recognized by the state, (2) the joining of man and woman in the eyes of God or (3) a competitive sport on network TV produced for the entertainment of millions? Anyone emerging recently from an isolation chamber (say, in Guantánamo Bay) might be forgiven for believing that marriage has gone to the dogs (and the gays and the lesbians, for that matter) and become a game show. Indeed, young men and women are lining up to be chosen by complete strangers for lifetime commitments even as divorce rates hover at 50 percent. Why has marriage become prime-time fodder for a public that craves escapist "reality" TV? Should we interpret these new marriage shows as evidence that the institution has completely crumbled or as a reinforcement of its ubiquity?

Reality marriage shows have angered conservatives who feel that the programs represent marriage as a kind of popularity contest. But one could easily argue that these shows take marriage for granted as a basic fact of life and revel in its endlessly fascinating details. Some gay and lesbian viewers have complained that these shows recentralize heterosexuality at a critical moment in the nation's marriage debates. And yet, the conservatives are ultimately right: *The Bachelor, Joe Millionaire, Average Joe, My Big Fat Obnoxious Fiancé* and all the other "win a husband/wife" shows surely trivialize the sanctity of marriage and, in the process, turn straight coupling, for better or for worse, into pure entertainment. Heterosexuality never looked so fragile.

The breakthrough marriage show was ABC's *The Bachelor,* which debuted in 2002. In the interests of gender equality, the successful first season was soon followed by its matched set: *The Bachelorette.* These shows set up the bachelor/ette with twenty-five dates and allow him or her to eliminate a certain number each week until the number of potential mates has been winnowed down to four. At this stage, the lucky bachelor/ette meets the suitors' families and then makes a cut. When the suitors have been reduced to the more wieldy number of three, the bachelor/ette goes on intimate overnighters with each date (creating an adulterous scenario in the process). After another cut, the two remaining contestants meet the bachelor/ette's family, and then he or she makes a final decision and proposes on the season's finale.

Reality TV Replaces Sitcoms

The reality marriage shows actually replace family sitcoms about the drudgery and necessary hardship of marriage (*Roseanne*) and challenge other sitcoms about the fun of single life (*Friends, Seinfeld, Sex and the City*). By giving marriage a radical makeover, they revive the audience's interest in private lives and turn the viewer's attention away from the public sphere during a period of intense political secrecy, grotesque military blunders and faint public dissent. The marriage shows, like much reality TV, produce a steady stream of "real" images of "conflict" (*Big Brother*), "survival" (*Survivor*) and "terror" (*Fear Factor*), which then compete with real conflict, real survival and real terror.

But don't mistake me for a reality-TV basher. Ever the cultural optimist, I truly believe that audiences can read between the lines of pure ideology (romance) to see clearly the actual rendering of marriage in these shows as practical (tax credits, access to sex, state recognition, gifts at the wedding, gifts at the baby shower, social and familial approval), while at the same time understand real marriage as neither romantic nor practical (little access to sex after a while, expensive to have children, you hate each others' family and friends).

In the end, *The Bachelor/ette* openly depicts heterosexual mating patterns in a Darwinian, "survival of the cutest" way, in which men and women choose mates based on looks and immediate sexual chemistry alone. This turns heterosexuality into a highly superficial system of selection that runs counter to the ideology of romance manufactured by Hollywood and women's magazines—namely the "soul mate" model, which, in fact, most of the participants on these shows bring with them. All of the marriage seekers claim to be open to love and marriage; all tend to be young, good-looking and financially secure; many, weirdly, seem to be in "pharmaceutical sales" (you tell me). Most claim to have been either unlucky in love or just not managing to find that one special person. Meredith

Phillips, for example, [the second] season's "bachelorette," says she signed up for the show "in an attempt to find her soul mate." Meredith, a makeup artist and a model, was a participant on Bob Guiney's season of *The Bachelor*. When Bob picked another hopeful lovely from his batch of ladies, Meredith was crushed, since she had been sure that Bob was her "soul mate." But ABC allowed her another stab at tracking down the elusive "one and only," and the next season she claimed to have found him among the twenty-five financially secure prospective husbands picked out for her perusal. Soulmate hunting, it turns out, depends less upon the twists and turns of fate and much more upon a well-funded boyfriend search on national TV.

A whole series of shows that followed *The Bachelor*, therefore, made it their mission to show that hetero men and women care about more than just money and looks. *Average Joe*, as the snappy title implies, asks a woman to choose from a set of "average guys," and *Joe Millionaire* has women compete for a guy whom they are tricked into thinking is very rich (in fact, he's a construction worker). While the goal of these parasite shows is to demonstrate that the participants really value relationships over fame, TV exposure, money and quick sexual encounters, in each case, greed and looks win out over other more abstract markers of compatibility. On *Average Joe*, for example, the producers send in a group of male models to confuse the bachelorette halfway through her process and, sure enough, each season, she jumps at one of the models and dumps the average Joes!

A Lack of Real Diversity

Reality shows, we now know, have a limited shelf life, in the sense that once the format has been learned by the audience, boredom can set in all too quickly. [One] season's *The Bachelor*, for instance, was so bad and so boring that you could not tell the difference between three out of the four final blond women, and the fourth was cast as a psycho around whom the producers engineered a very halfhearted stalking episode.

Are the shows trying to caution against interracial unions or just portray a process of 'natural selection' as 'color-blind?'

The tedium factor drove all the networks to new creative lows this season, and they desperately fiddled with the format to try to find fresh arrangements of groomed male and female bodies in search of matrimony. So, audiences could pick between *My Big Fat Obnoxious Fiance, The Littlest Groom* and even a gay show on Bravo, *Boy Meets Boy*. On the first, a woman has to trick her parents into accepting her "big fat obnoxious" fiancé, who is played by a professional actor, in order to win a million dollars. In the second, a midget man picks between a group of female small people and some regular-sized women. And in the gay version, a clean-cut, handsome and smart white gay guy goes on dates with countless other clean-cut, handsome and smart white guys (only some of whom are actually gay) in search of a life partner. His challenge is to select the gay men from the gay impersonators. *My Big Fat Blah, Blah, Blah* failed because the trickery was staged and blatant; the midget marriage series bombed because it exposed the "freak show" aspect of all the marriage shows. And the "trick the fag" show ultimately fell way short of its aspirations because the gay contestants, in the end, seemed far more interested in cruising each other than in focusing their attention on the one good-looking gay guy selected by producers as the Prime Gay!

Two scenarios have so far been completely avoided by the "get hitched in prime time" phenomenon. First, all the shows have refused to test the waters of interracial dating, and so far none have cast a bachelor/ette of color in the main role. In a perfunctory nod to diversity, there are always contestants of color in the group of potential mates at the beginning of these shows. The black or Asian contestants usually don't make it past the third round (you don't want to cut them too quickly); the occasional ambiguous Latina/o can make it a bit further. But in the end, these shows always manage to avoid parading interracial romance on prime time. A suspicious viewer might be inclined to read intimations of social engineering into these shows. Are they ads for white families at a time when demographic shifts have made white people a minority in certain cities and states? Are the shows trying to caution against interracial unions or just portray a process of "natural selection" as "color-blind?"

Few of the hopefuls on reality marriage shows actually marry their new mates.

Second, while the format seems to extend to telegenic gay dudes, so far there is no interest in creating a show about lesbian dating/mating. Far be it from me to advocate for such a thing, given that, based upon *The L Word*, such a show would undoubtedly involve hetero-looking bisexual babes pressing up against each other for the viewing pleasures of straight men. And yet, the absence of lesbians and people of color (not to mention lesbians of color) bears mentioning. Apparently, US audiences can thrill to the spectacle of arranged marriages and dating opportunities for all kinds of white and heterosexual bodies, but the whiff of interracial or lesbian trysts would make audiences queasy and stretch the marriage paradigm to its limit.

The Nonreality of Reality TV Dating

On the finale of *Average Joe Hawaii*, one bachelor finally took a stand and rejected his new mate in a fit of pique. Was he reacting to the false moralism of the show? Was he refusing to fall in love in three days on national TV? Did he want to make a point about selling intimacy short? Nope, he was furious that his new girlfriend had held back from him a frightening secret: She had once dated Fabio! Even though no one could explain why this "secret" should bother our "Above Average Joe," he claimed that "any guy in America" would feel as outraged as he did. What Fabio represented to this insecure model-actor we may never know, but these are the mysteries of reality TV that we must tolerate. In the end, our stud could not recover from this terrible disclosure, and the match made in NBC studios faltered and died a natural death.

Few of the hopefuls on reality marriage shows actually marry their new mates. Most use their time in the limelight to secure modeling contracts, get exposure as actors and enjoy the half-light of the semi-celebrity status that chases them for a few weeks after the show ends. Of course, if they were honest, the studs and babes would admit that the chance to nuzzle, cuddle and smooch twenty-five hotties with impunity in a two-month span is reason enough to sign on for the rocky ride of reality dating. But honesty is not the best policy for bachelor/ettes. So as each potential soul mate confesses to "falling for" (the most overused phrase in reality marriage land) the man or woman of the hour, the bachelor/ette returns the love and longing in equal measure and commits to love, honor and obey, forsaking all others, in sickness and in health, until death do they part, or at least until the next episode.

10

Reality TV Promotes a Democratic View of Society

Kira Cochrane

Kira Cochrane is an editor for the Guardian, *British newspaper, and writes a regular column in the British newsmagazine* New Statesman.

While reality TV may have shortcomings, critics who complain of the poor quality of programs are elitist. Reality TV participants represent a greater diversity than one usually finds in television programming, including participants who are disabled, transsexual, and overweight. Even when reality TV programs display the prejudiced behavior of contestants or viewers voting from home, they nonetheless offer an accurate (and thus critical) portrait of society's limitations.

So reality TV is crap, its viewers are chumps and its participants are talentless wannabes?

Consider a few recent stories. After preview screenings of the film *Dreamgirls*, the singer Jennifer Hudson was hailed as a "megawatt talent" by US critics. Hudson's big break? The reality TV show *American Idol*. In *Dreamgirls*, for her first ever film role, Hudson shares the screen with stars such as Eddie Murphy, Jamie Foxx and Beyoncé Knowles. All these actors have been praised for their performances, but only Hudson is seen as an Oscar shoo-in [Hudson did win the 2007 Oscar].

Then there's Connie Fisher, winner of the British talent show *How Do You Solve a Problem Like Maria?*. It was derided by actors and critics, who deemed it outrageous to use a TV programme to cast the leading lady in *The Sound of Music.* Fast-forward to Fisher's West End debut, where she was acclaimed as one of the most talented stars in musical history.

Next comes Leona Lewis, the breathy balladeer wowing the judges on *The X Factor.* She's apparently already been asked on to a top-rated American talk show, suggesting she might succeed where almost all recent UK acts have failed: conquering the US market.

To say that reality TV serves up nothing but dross is nonsense. I'm more than willing to allow that it has offered us some pretty dumb, even horrific, spectacles—including David Beckham's alleged mistress Rebecca Loos "pleasuring" a pig, and the diet expert Gillian McKeith poking around in human excrement.

Many who deride reality TV were born not necessarily with a silver spoon in their mouth, but with their foot firmly in the door.

Reality TV has also veered towards stereotype in its casting. The diversity of female contestants on *Big Brother,* for instance, has all but disappeared. Of the five women left in the house halfway through [2006]'s show, four had breast implants and the fifth was a former Miss Wales. These flaws are the fault of blinkered producers. The more significant fact is that, since the current strain of reality TV hit our screens in 2000, it has proved a democratic triumph.

Reality TV Promotes Diversity

In a world still obsessed with the thin, the rich, the straight and the perfectly groomed, it has made stars of the most unlikely people—fat singers (Michelle McManus on *Pop Idol*), Portuguese transsexuals (Nadia Almada on *Big Brother*), even double-glazing salespeople (*The Armstrongs*).

It has also made visible the most ignored minority in the country: the disabled. This year's stars have included Kerry McGregor, a wheelchair-using *X Factor* contestant, and Pete Bennett, the popular *Big Brother* winner (who happens to have Tourette's syndrome). To say that either should have been protected from the experience is just bloody patronising.

I've always suspected that many who deride reality TV were born not necessarily with a silver spoon in their mouth, but with their foot firmly in the door. One of the reasons these programmes are so disliked by the elite is that they showcase the stories and experiences of people who aren't "supposed" to be on television—the poor, the suburban, the rural.

Aside from the lame celebrity spin-off shows, reality TV stars aren't people with well-connected parents. They're not the SADOS ("sons and daughters of stars") who prance at society parties and make up *Tatler's Little Black Book* of eligible folk. No, those who participate in reality shows have reached the screen because they are talented, or entertaining, or both. It's easy to portray contestants as wannabes, desperate for fame, unprepared for graft, but the truth is quite different. Connie Fisher, Leona Lewis and Will Young, for example, committed themselves to years of drama and music training. And yet, despite a clutch of scholarships and prizes between them, none had that final contact that would have got them noticed. Most people don't.

In 2000, when *Big Brother* was in its infancy, it seemed that appearing on such shows might ruin people's lives. Those first programmes had that potential. Contestants then were largely unaware of how the medium operated. Now the participants are well versed and there are remarkably few complaints.

[In 2005], Trevor Phillips spoke up for the genre, saying that by featuring many black, Asian and other ethnic-minority participants, it challenged racial stereotypes. This is true. Also true, and much less satisfying, is the fact that the winners chosen by the British public so far have all been white. Yet we can't blame this on the programmes.

In reflecting our racism back at us, they arguably provide a service. If there is one thing that would make me even fonder of reality TV, it would be to see this trend bucked. There's only one thing for it, people—rise up, and vote Leona!

11

Reality TV Can Motivate Generosity Across America

Sara B. Miller and Amanda Paulson

Sara B. Miller and Amanda Paulson are staff writers for the Christian Science Monitor.

While observers have accused reality TV of pandering to the lowest common denominator, the best of these programs may help motivate America to better the lives of those who need it most. From building homes for needy families to extreme makeovers for individuals, Reality TV shows can improve morale across America and give hope to those in most need for the future.

Brand new Pontiac G6s for an entire audience, many of whom desperately need a car. A reality show that not only builds a family a new house, but mends the problems within, from weight loss to relationships. And in the Catskills of upstate New York, an entire town gets a makeover, giving a community "a new place to call home."

Television, it seems, is showing its softer side.

Tucked amid the back-stabbing and maggot-eating fests like "Survivor" or "Fear Factor" that are the staples of reality TV, comes a bevy of feel-good, life-improving shows determined to leave their targets—or at least appear to leave them—better than they found them.

The rise in Good Samaritan TV is, in part, a backlash against the skullduggery that has made its way into family living rooms in recent years. But it also plays into a powerful market desire for make-over in America. The country is fascinated with both the notion of reinvention and the philanthropic vehicle often used to get there—as was seen by the buzz generated when Oprah Winfrey handed out 276 sets of keys donated by General Motors, a gesture worth some $7 million.

Don't worry, though: Those who still want the manipulation and scheming of shows like "Big Brother" can certainly find it. They can watch participants humiliate themselves in any number of ways.

Indeed, reality TV came of age using a winner-takes-all model, says Toby Miller, director of the Film and Visual Culture program at the University of California in Riverside. Now it is trying to increase its staying power with a jolt of variety.

"This is, in a sense, a slight turn away from the harshness of that Darwinian world that you see exemplified in 'Survivor' or 'Dr. Phil,' toward something a little sweeter or nicer," he says.

But the shows also play into two long-time fascinations for Americans: philanthropy and the remade life.

Helping Those that Need It Most

Do-good TV, of course, is hardly revolutionary. Makeover shows and programs that lavish unexpected bounty on participants have been around since the beginning of television. In the 1950s, "It Could Be You" reunited audience members with long-lost relatives on air, while "Strike it Rich," the self-proclaimed "quiz show with a heart," took down-on-their luck contestants who, if unable to answer the questions, could call the "heart line" and get donations from viewers.

The format still has a market today. "Home Delivery," a new daytime offering from NBC Universal, bills itself as "part makeover, part talk show, and part reality with heart." Its four hosts travel the country, taking their cameras into peoples' homes and finding ways to "transform" their subjects' lives, usually with a showering of gifts: corrective surgery for a boy born without ears, or new uniforms and tickets to Broadway for a New Haven drill team.

For a new Fox show, "Renovate My Family," producers sought not only families in need of home repair but with serious challenges hindering their psychological progress, like obesity or addiction. And on Sony TV's "Moving In," self-help guru and former 76ers owner Pat Croce parks his Winnebago in peoples' driveway for a day, offering not gifts but advice—every life-affirming, 12-step trick he knows.

Inspiring America

Part of the reason for the onslaught of new "feel good" shows comes from the success of more warm-hearted reality offerings like "Queer Eye for the Straight Guy" and the many home and fashion makeover shows.

"Once a company touches a nerve with the American people and shows the rest of the industry this is what America likes, other networks begin to copy it," says TV historian Fred MacDonald.

But the shows also play into two long-time fascinations for Americans: philanthropy and the remade life. "The United States specializes in the makeover," says Dr. Miller. "The Macy's hatcheck girl who becomes a movie star is part of the grand mythology. What you're seeing now in the makeover shows is a reaching back into the rich lode of that myth."

Reality TV Generosity Too Good to Be True?

Back in the 1950s, "Strike it Rich" ultimately became a problem, says Mr. MacDonald, because so many hard-up people began moving to New York with nothing, hoping for a chance to get on the show.

That's a similar criticism that some find in today's programs as well. Some call it flagrant marketing that takes advantage of the less fortunate. "It's really cheap. It exploits their emotional reactions as they squeal and holler and look like little kids at Christmas," says James Weaver, a professor of communication and psychology at Virginia Tech in Blacksburg.

And he questions the long-term value of such giving. Instead of building a new home for a family, questions Mr. Weaver, wouldn't it be better to teach that same family how to renovate their own home?

For Ed Justus, the mayor of Jeffersonville, the Catskills town of 420 in the midst of transformation, the effects can be lasting. Most of the plans of the Learning Channel in a new series set to air in January called "Town Haul" are top-secret. But Mr. Justus say they are building a teen center, beautifying local businesses, and renovating a building to accommodate a handicapped resident.

"I was gung-ho right from the start," Justus says. "It will put us on the map. I think in years to come people will talk about Jeffersonville."

After all, reality TV is a form of dramatic art.

Such shows, with hope and change at their foundation, can play better with audiences than makeover shows where fame and fortune alone are the prizes, says Robert Thompson, a media expert at Syracuse University in upstate New York.

Inspiration of Quality Reality TV Gives Hope to the Future

That might be especially true today. While television is often used as an escape, some say terrorism, the war in Iraq, and joblessness make "nice" more appealing. "We are feeling so vulnerable and endangered, so worried about the future, there is a kind of drive to do something good and do it fast," says Faith Popcorn, a marketing trend watcher.

But critics say that salaciousness is likely to remain a staple, at least on prime-time television. Most of the more benign programs can be found on cable networks and during day-time syndication, while the night is still committed to "wheeling and dealing," says Professor Thompson. "The very same audience that might really like a good knockdown dragout fight on 'The Apprentice'" he says, also delights in "the dream come true."

After all, reality TV is a form of dramatic art. "Conflict creates drama, and villains create conflict," says Ed Robertson, a pop culture critic in California. "Nice isn't very dramatic. Unless you're Oprah."

12

Reality TV Appeals to Baser Instincts

Douglas Rushkoff

Douglas Rushkoff is a New York-based writer, columnist, and lecturer on technology, media, and popular culture.

A famous psychological experiment encouraged participants to issue shocks to test subjects. The idea was to find out if participants would follow orders, even when these orders included inflicting pain on others (while the shocks in the experiment were not real, the participants believed they were). While the American Psychological Association declared these experiments unethical in 1973, the experiments have more or less morphed into a new and perhaps unlikely form: reality TV. Basically, the viewer tunes into reality TV to watch contestants who are willing to suffer any hardship and/or shame in order to appear on television. Although viewers feel guilty for enjoying another person's suffering, advertisers, by supporting the program, offer an endorsement of the proceedings. In this way, advertisers win the viewers' confidence by sublimating their self-loathing. Viewers, finally, are reluctant to take responsibility for the hardships of reality TV participants; without the viewers, though, the programs would not exist.

We thought they had ended over 40 years ago, but Stanley Milgram's infamous psychology experiments are back—in a crueler and more public form than he ever devised.

Douglas Rushkoff, "Who Are the Real Subjects of the Psychology Experiments We Call Reality TV?" *Discover*, vol. 28, May 2007, p. 75. Copyright 2007 Discover Media LLC. Reproduced by permission.

The original experiments were inspired by the Nuremberg trial of Adolf Eichmann, who engineered the transport of Jews to Nazi concentration camps, Milgram wanted to know if German war criminals could have simply been "following orders," as they claimed, and not truly complicit in the death camp atrocities. To find out, he set up an experiment in which subjects were instructed by men in white lab coats to deliver increasingly intense electric shocks to victims who screamed in pain, complained of a heart condition, and begged for the experiment to be halted. More than half of the subjects carried out the orders despite their own mounting anxiety, slowly increasing the electric shocks to seemingly lethal levels. Although they were later informed that their victims were just actors, the subjects suffered lasting psychological trauma after discovering just what they themselves were capable of. (Such experiments were declared unethical by the American Psychological Association in 1973.)

Now researchers at University College London are delicately recreating Milgram's work using computer-generated characters instead of actors. The subjects still "shock" their victims, who still scream in pain, but this time everyone knows it's only as real as a video game. Yet while the victims are obviously fake, the subjects exhibit the same anxiety about inflicting pain, as measured by self-reports, requests to stop the experiment, and increased heart rate and sweating. The study's authors proudly conclude that "this result reopens the door to direct empirical studies of obedience and related extreme social situations, an area of research that is otherwise not open to experimental study."

I find it odd, though, that scientists should go to such lengths to create virtual characters for human subjects to torture. Really, there's no need, when every night on prime-time television we can find experiments involving similarly "extreme social situations" being carried out on real human beings—subjects willing to submit to the most debasing forms of public humiliation Hollywood executives can dream up.

Reality TV as Interpersonal Torture

Yes, I'm talking about reality TV, an ongoing experiment in interpersonal torture that, even more than the University College London study, picks up where Milgram left off. This time around, the location (be it a French chateau or South Sea island) is the laboratory, the contestants are the subjects, and the producers are the lab-coated scientists—using the authority of their cameras to push participants to ever more exhibitionist, vile, or self-destructive lengths. Although essentially unscripted, reality shows are nonetheless constructed; they are setups with clear hypotheses, designed to maximize the probability of conflict and embarrassment.

America's Next Top Model is not really about who wins a modeling contract but rather about observing what young anorexics are willing to do to one another under the sanctioning authority of supermodel Tyra Banks. Will they steal food, sabotage another contestant's makeup, or play particularly vicious mind games? *Survivor* has never been about human ingenuity in the face of nature but about human scheming, betrayal, and selfishness in the course of competition. And *The Surreal World*, which throws a bunch of has-beens and recovering alcoholic former child stars into a halfway house, has nothing to do with our desire to emulate celebrities. It's about watching sad people sacrifice any remaining vestige of self-respect to garner an extra few minutes of life on the tube.

Sooner or later those of us feasting on this orgy of tele-sadism will have to accept our complicity in the process.

The disturbing part is that we call this entertainment. Milgram was hoping to learn something basically uplifting: History's worst sadists were in fact decent human beings, just highly susceptible to the corrupting influence of authorities. What reality TV proves about us is far worse. Apparently, we're just waiting for an excuse to be true to our darkest natures.

Who Is Responsible for Reality TV?

Sooner or later those of us feasting on this orgy of tele-sadism will have to accept our complicity in the process. After all, in Milgram's experiments the real subjects were not the recipients of the electric shocks but those administering them. As the virtual reality versions have proved, it doesn't matter whether what's happening is real or staged: We react as if the pain inflicted were real. By sitting still for the elaborately staged social experiments of reality TV, we supply further evidence for Milgram's main conclusion: "Ordinary people . . . without any particular hostility on their part, can become agents in a terrible destructive process."

Yet with no white-coated experimenter sitting in our living rooms, who is the ultimate authority figure granting us permission to delight in the pain of others? Who absolves us of our guilt? Why the sponsor, of course, whose ad for a wholesome national brand interrupts at just the right moment, stamping events with its seal of approval. Sponsors of reality programs gain leverage over their viewers by warding off our sense of shame. Note that viewers are not willing to pay directly for these shows on HBO. They're available only on free TV, where advertisers assume culpability on our behalf.

Just like subjects in the Milgram experiments, we may soon come to realize, with painful and soul-shaking clarity, what it is that we have done. The self-loathing of the principal subjects awaits us.

13

Reality TV Encourages a Negative Body Image

Dana Stevens

Dana Stevens is a movie critic for Slate, *an online magazine.*

When Reality TV programs started receiving complaints that they were discriminating against gay participants, they decided to find a new group to discriminate against: the overweight. Strangely, these programs express a troubling ambiguity toward weight: while these shows encourage participants to lose weight, their very premise depends on overweight contestants. In some cases the programs have tied emotional rewards to food, seemingly handicapping the participants' effort to lose weight; in others, overweight individuals have been pitted against thinner contestants in unfair competitions. Despite these problems, these shows remain popular, reflecting the ambiguity that Americans feel about their own weight problems.

On reality television, fat people are the new gay people. Earlier [in 2004], Fox was forced to cancel two gay-themed reality shows, the short-lived *Playing It Straight* and the never-aired *Seriously Dude, I'm Gay*, due to protests from advocacy groups and general viewer indifference. These shows, which I discussed in a *Slate* article at the time, exploited cultural fears about homosexuality by making gay men the "wild card" in traditional reality-show competitions. To their credit, audiences responded with a shrug. But the evil forces that plot new reality shows have now turned their attention to a new sideshow attraction: the overweight.

Reality television has chosen [the fall 2004] season to mine the American obsession with body size. *The Biggest Loser*, a weight-loss-themed reality series in which two teams of dieters, the "reds" and the "blues," compete to see who can lose the most pounds per week, has been expanded from an hour to an hour and a half per week. VH1's *Flab to Fab* . . . subjects overweight fans to the diet and exercise regimens of their favorite celebrities. . . . And Showtime's *Fat Actress* . . . is already being widely publicized as a comedy/reality hybrid in which Kirstie Alley, playing herself, seeks to overcome Hollywood's prejudice against large women and jump-start her television career. Finally, there's Toccara, who, until she was voted off the show . . . was the "plus-sized" anomaly among the svelte beauties on [2004]'s *America's Next Top Model.* . . .

All of these shows share a deep ambivalence toward excess flesh, seeking to eliminate it even as they depend on it for their very existence. The title of *The Biggest Loser* says it all: The more you lose, the more you win, but even if you take first place, you're still a loser. While television executives may be congratulating themselves on their inclusiveness, they have created reality programming that capitalizes on Americans' fear and hatred of their bodies, making the differently sized the stars of a freak show.

A Cruel Season Line-Up

In . . . [a] video clip promoting *Fat Actress*, for example, Alley systematically works away at a huge plate of spaghetti as she explains the show's premise: For every 5 pounds she loses, she will be allowed to stay on the air an additional week. Alley can have her spaghetti and eat it, too—she can be fat and still be a TV star—but only if she is willing to make her weight the sole focus of the show. The Showtime Web site for *Fat Actress* lauds Alley as "bravely willing to lampoon her image," which, the press release goes on to cluck disapprovingly, has been "mercilessly ridiculed over the past few years." It's hard not to hear the self-congratulatory hypocrisy in this formulation—isn't *Fat Actress* just another form of the same merciless ridicule?

The Biggest Loser, which at its new hour-and-a-half length is more desperately in need of slimming than its subjects, takes that hypocrisy to a new level. The vast majority of screen time is taken up by shots of the 12 hefty candidates in skimpy bathing suits and tank tops, clambering over obstacle courses or submitting themselves to abject "challenges." A segment called "Oversized Pop Star" asks the teams to sing about their weight struggles in front of an audience. These contests are billed as a chance for the participants to strut their spunky self-esteem, but for all the carefully rehearsed pride, there's no question that the show's organizing principles are voyeurism and humiliation. In one of [a November 2004 episode's] challenges, the red team was presented with a gooey cinnamon roll and a telephone and told that whoever consumed the roll would be allowed a phone call home. The way this trick was set up—if you eat the treat, you get to make the phone call—was particularly diabolical in that it equated gastronomic deprivation with emotional restraint and face-stuffing with familial love.

America's Next Top Model is crueler in its treatment of its participants. Many of the *Top Model* "challenges," for example, blatantly handicap heavier women; [in a November 2004 episode], a demonic stylist set the women loose in a designer department store and gave them 15 minutes to come up with a "head-to-toe look." Toccara, visibly stymied by the challenge of finding chic clothes in sizes 12 to 14, meandered glumly among the racks while her slim competitors raced to and fro, accumulating multiple options. "I was a little worried about Toccara because her pace was very slow," sniffed the stylist afterward, conveniently ignoring the sizing issue. When Toccara was voted off at the end of the episode (for reasons that the usually ruthless hostess Tyra Banks seemed unable to articulate), she gamely tried to rationalize her role on the show as a trailblazer for large women in fashion: "I'm just grateful that maybe I made a path for someone else." Unfortunately, Toccara's role at times seemed more like that of the sacrificial calf. Enormously popular with fans of the show, she was nonetheless doomed to be voted off; it was as if Toccara simultaneously represented the identification with larger-sized bodies and the cultural need to punish those who possess them.

Flab to Fab combines the celebrity aspirations of the beauties on *America's Next Top Model* with the self-loathing of the dieters on *The Biggest Loser*. But the women who participate in this hourlong competitive workout show don't need supermodels and stylists to belittle them; they can do it all by themselves. "I can't believe I go out in public looking like this," moaned Angelique, a perfectly presentable, if chubby, young woman who was one of the three contestants on [a November 2004] show. Another, Victoria, wept as she blamed her weight for her romantic difficulties: "I'm 32 years old, and I'm alone." Lachrecia, the heaviest of the three at 190 pounds, seemed painfully aware of her status as an object for the viewing audience's vicarious disgust. In an interview segment after her initial weigh-in, her self-assessment is strangely depersonalized: "A person that weighs 190 pounds and has 43 percent body fat is someone I see on TV or on the street and think: I'm nothing like them."

Each of these series is careful not to overtly mock its participants, but that hasn't stopped the press from doing so— one reviewer suggested that the red and blue teams on *The Biggest Loser* rename themselves the "Butter Buddies" and the "Lard Lovers." Given that around 64 percent of the American population is overweight, one wonders what kind of masochistic schadenfreude [satisfaction from the misfortunes of others] is behind the success of these shows.

14

Reality TV Can Promote a Positive Body Image

Willow Bay

Willow Bay is a former fashion model and an editor with the Huffington Post.

One of the most troubling trends in health has been the rise in childhood obesity. One reality TV program, Shaq's Big Challenge, *works directly with overweight children in an effort to reverse this trend, helping children learn new habits through fitness training. By showing the everyday struggles of six children who are overweight, the program will offer life lessons to other children who watch the program. While Shaq's Big Challenge hopes to make a difference in the childhood obesity epidemic, its architect, basketball star Shaquille O'Neal, realizes that the program only offers one piece of a very difficult puzzle: parents, guardians, and schools will also need to participate.*

NBA superstar Shaquille O'Neal is using his super-sized (7-foot 1 inch, 325 pounds) persona, his credibility as a four-time NBA champion, and the platform of a reality TV series to launch a "Shaq Attack" on the nation's childhood obesity epidemic.

In *Shaq's Big Challenge* six "dangerously obese" Broward County, Florida middle school children spend six months shedding pounds, improving their eating habits, and, if the first two shows are any indication, learning—the hard way—to exercise. In the role of motivator-in-chief, O'Neal has assembled his own "dream team" of doctors, trainers, coaches and nutritionists to work with his recruits. Given the enormity of the mental and physical challenges these children face, they will need the team's expertise and support.

My boys (ages 8 and 4), rabid NBA fans, were begging to watch "Shaq's show." And superstar that he is, Shaq didn't disappoint. He had them from the first scene. After watching the kids struggle with their fitness test, my little one spent the rest of the night doing push-ups. And they've both been asking to watch some more. What's most appealing about the series is Shaq's easy—and sometimes goofy—way with the boys and girls. He has six children of his own, and is a bit of a big kid himself. (In one scene, he advises Walter, who is being teased at school, to "go punch those boys right in the face." Then, almost in slow motion, we see the adult take over. Shaq pauses, shakes his head, and then takes it back). The program also offers a fascinating glimpse into the ways in which well-intentioned and clearly loving parents both deny the seriousness of the problem, and enable unhealthy behavior, even after Shaq's dream team intervenes.

In terms of the show's approach to physical fitness, I would have preferred to see a little less boot camp and a bit more emphasis on the mind-body connection. But hey, it's only week two, and they've all got a lot to learn.

This is the first generation predicted to have a shorter lifespan than their parents.

In his battle against childhood obesity, O'Neal is thinking big. His ultimate goal is to create a fitness plan for Florida—where the State Department of Health estimates 25 percent of children are obese or at risk of becoming obese—that can serve as a model for the entire country. On Shaq's to-do list: push Florida to implement mandatory physical education courses for middle school and high school students. As of now, it's offered in only six percent of schools. "That's disgusting!" says Shaq. I caught up with O'Neal briefly by email the day he met with Florida's Governor, Charlie Crist, at a rally for 500 students to encourage children and young adults to adopt healthy eating habits and daily physical activity.

Tackling Childhood Obesity

Willow Bay: In the first show, a doctor says of you, "He cares. That's the key, he cares." Why did you take on this issue in such a personal way? And why tackle childhood obesity with a TV series?

Shaquille O'Neal: When I first saw the data that indicated how serious the issue of childhood obesity is, I knew that I had to get involved. First, as a parent, and as someone who has always had a special connection with young people, I was amazed at the current health trends. If I can in any way be a part of making things better for kids—who are our future— then I felt like I had a responsibility to do that. The television show hopefully is a good way to take the message directly to people in the comfort of their homes.

How bad is the problem? And how do the children you are working with on the show reflect that?

Here are the statistics that jumped out at me: This is the first generation predicted to have a shorter lifespan than their parents. Childhood obesity numbers have tripled in the last 20 years in the U.S.; and nearly one-third of U.S. children, 25 million of them, are overweight or nearly overweight. The kids in the show are great kids. Their health challenges result from the same things that affect kids around the country— they are basically inactive, and they eat unhealthy foods in disproportionate amounts. The reasons why they are inactive or eat unhealthily may vary, and you see some of that in the show.

You say, "In each kid I see a little bit of myself." That's hard for us to imagine; what do you see in them that feels familiar to you?

It will take parents, guardians, school boards and children themselves to reverse the trends.

Well, first, I was always bigger than kids my age, so I understand what it feels like to be separated by size. And if it wasn't for athletics, I very well may have been an obese kid. But I also saw how some of these kids felt like outsiders. For them, it was because their self-esteem was affected by how they looked or how other kids treated them based on how they looked. In my life, I often felt like an outsider for various reasons—whether it was moving around a lot as a military kid, my size, whatever.

We all have our weakness when it comes to food, what's yours?

Sandwiches. I have to watch the carb intake.

Any surprises for you in all of this?

Yes. I didn't realize that it would be so hard. You read the statistics and you hear stuff, but getting involved with a real group of kids and their families shows you all of the complexities. I brought in a great team of experts, because we needed to address this in a thorough way.

What kind of impact do you hope to have . . . on these children and others?

I just hope that I can help them and families across the country live healthier lives. I'm just one person doing a small part. I can't solve childhood obesity. It will take parents, guardians, school boards and children themselves to reverse the trends. I'm just hoping to get the message out, along with some useful information that may make it easier.

15

Reality TV Allows Viewers to Live Vicariously (performed)

Cynthia M. Frisby

Cynthia M. Frisby is an associate professor of advertising at the University of Missouri–Columbia School of Journalism.

Americans love reality TV, and this love affair extends beyond voyeurism and pure entertainment. In essence, reality TV allows viewers to live vicariously, experiencing the joys, pains, and fears of others. Social comparison theory states that people build identity and cope with problems by comparing their lives with those of others. Reality TV allows viewers to compare themselves with ordinary people who—through the program—participate in extraordinary events, sometimes in exotic locations. As viewers experience the exotic in their own lives through reality TV shows, many also experience mood enhancement. Most Americans will never appear on reality TV, but they can do the next best thing: compare themselves with and live through the experiences of participants who are just like they are.

Every year, television networks vie to create cutting edge programming. New shows promise more drama, suspense, and laughter while pushing the envelope of what is morally and socially acceptable, funny, thrilling, and, of course, entertaining. Fitting all these criteria—at least according to the soaring ratings—is reality based television.

Reality TV is a genre of programming in which the everyday routines of "real life" people (as opposed to fictional char-

Cynthia M. Frisby, "Getting Real With Reality TV," *USA Today*, vol. 133, September 2004, pp. 50–54. Copyright © 2004 Society for the Advancement of Education. Reproduced by permission.

acters played by actors) are followed closely by the cameras. Viewers cannot seem to help but become involved in the captivating plotlines and day-to-day drama depicted daily on their screens. Apparently, people simply take pleasure in watching other people's lives while those under scrutiny enjoy being on television enough to go on for free.

There are three major categories within the reality genre: game shows (e.g., *Survivor*), dating shows (e.g., *The Bachelor*), and talent shows (e.g., *American Idol*). While reality programming breeds fiercely during the regular season, in summer there is an even greater glut since such programs are cheap to produce and, if they fail to draw ratings, they quickly can be flushed away and replaced with something else.

It is becoming increasingly difficult to avoid contact with reality TV these days. In offices, hair salons, health clubs, restaurants, and bars, the general public is discussing what happened on television the night before—and it is not the world news they are dissecting. Rather, the hot topic may be what happened on *The Apprentice*. Then again, it might be a "did-you-see" conversation concerning *The Bachelor* or *For Love or Money*.

America's Love Affair with Reality TV

Shows such as *The Apprentice, Survivor, Fear Factor, The Amazing Race, American Idol, American Girl, Big Brother, Extreme Makeover, Temptation Island, Cheaters, The Simple Life, Queer Eye for the Straight Guy, The Bachelor*, and *The Bachelorette* have reached out and grabbed today's American television viewer. During the 2003–04 season, 10 reality shows ranked among the top 25 prime-time programs in the audience-composition index for adults 18–49 with incomes of $75,000 or more. Nielsen ratings indicate that more than 18,000,000 viewers have been captivated by television programs that take ordinary people and place them in situations that have them competing in ongoing contests while being filmed 24 hours a day. What is it about these shows that attracts millions of loyal viewers week after week? Is it blatant voyeurism, or can their success be explained as a harmless desire for entertainment?

From *Survivor*, to *Elimidate* to *Average Joe*, to *Joe Millionaire*, it seems that reality TV succeeds because it plays off of real-life concerns—looking for love, competing to win a job or big prize, or becoming a millionaire—situations (or dreams) that most people can relate to. However, as these shows become more pervasive, their grip on "reality" seems to be growing more tenuous.

"It's refreshing to see everyday people getting some of the spotlight, rather than just seeing movie stars all the time," maintains CBS News associate Presley Weir. According to CBS, the same element of being human that encourages people to gossip about the lives of their friends, family, and even total strangers is what fosters an audience for reality television. Much like a car crash on the side of the freeway, glimpses into the interior workings of other human beings is often shocking, yet impossible to turn away from. It was this theory that produced MTV's *The Real World*, often referred to as "the forerunner of reality television shows." Seven strangers are selected to live together, and viewers watch to find out what happens when individuals with different backgrounds and points of view are left in close quarters.

Social Comparison Theory

Researchers frequently refer to at least six gratifications of media use: information (also known as surveillance or knowledge), escape, passing time, entertainment, social viewing/status enhancement, and relaxation. Although the names or labels for these gratifications may change, various studies confirm that they hold up in and across all situations. So what type of gratifications do viewers receive from reality TV?

Social comparison theory may help to explain and uncover an important motive—which many people may be unable, or unwilling, to express openly—for watching reality television. Psychologists define social comparison as "the process of thinking about information about one or more people in relation to the self." Social comparison theory postulates that individuals have a drive or need to compare their abilities and opinions to others. In 1954, [social psychologist] Leon Festinger, who coined the theory and pioneered research in this area, believed that people who are uncertain about their abilities and opinions will evaluate themselves by making comparisons with similar others.

Actually, individuals compare themselves with others for a variety of reasons, including to: determine relative standing on an issue or related ability; emulate behaviors; determine norms; lift spirits or feel better about life and personal situations; and evaluate emotions, personality, and self-worth.

Those made with others who are superior to or better off than oneself are referred to as upward comparisons. Individuals engaging in upward comparison may learn from others, be inspired by their examples, and become highly motivated to achieve similar goals. Upward comparisons, research suggests, are invoked when a person is motivated to change or overcome difficulties. Self-improvement is the main effect of an upward comparison because the targets serve as role models, teaching and motivating individuals to achieve or overcome similar problems.

On the other hand, when a social comparison involves a target who is inferior, incompetent, or less fortunate, it is referred to as a downward comparison. Its basic principle is that people feel better about their own situation and enhance their subjective well-being when they make comparisons with others who are worse off. Supposedly, downward comparisons help individuals cope with personal problems by allowing them to see themselves and their difficulties in a more positive light by realizing there are others who face more difficult circumstances.

Reality TV allows audiences to laugh, cry, and live vicariously through so-called everyday, ordinary people.

A social comparison does not mean that the individual has to give careful, elaborate, conscious thought about the comparison, but implies that there has to be, to some degree, an attempt to identify or look for similarities or differences between the other and self on some particular dimension. There are theorists who might argue that, for a comparison to be considered a comparison, the individual must be aware of the comparison and come into direct contact with the other person. However, psychologists have discovered that social comparisons do not require conscious or direct personal contact because fictional characters illustrated in the media can represent meaningful standards of comparison.

Gratification and Reality TV

Data on social comparisons and media use suggest that everyday encounters with media images may provide viewers with information that encourages them to engage in an automatic, spontaneous social comparison. This ultimately affects mood and other aspects of subjective well-being. People just might not be able to articulate consciously the comparison process or consciously register its effects (*i.e.*, self-enhancement, self-improvement, etc.).

Reality TV allows audiences to laugh, cry, and live vicariously through so-called everyday, ordinary people who have opportunities to experience things that, until the moment they are broadcast, most individuals only dream about. Viewers may tune into these shows: because they contain elements the audience would like to experience themselves; to laugh at the mistakes of others and/or celebrate successes; or to feel better about themselves because they are at least not as "bad as the people on television."

Exposure to tragic events or bad news invites social comparison among viewers. It is believed that reality audiences may be encouraged to compare and contrast their own situation with those of the reality show stars, and that this comparison process eventually could produce a form of self-satisfaction.

In real-life, everyday situations, it would be extremely difficult to avoid making some type of comparison. Frequently, people may compare themselves with others in their immediate environment or in the mass media in order to judge their own personal worth.

Reality TV and mood enhancement

We contacted 110 people and asked them to complete a uses and gratifications survey on reality television with two goals in mind: to demonstrate that social comparisons may be elicited by certain television content and to explore if viewers use reality television's content and images as a source for social comparison.

Of the respondents, 78.2% reported being regular viewers of reality television programs. A list of 37 reality shows was presented to the participants. They were asked to check those that they watch on a regular basis, and indicate on a scale of 1–5—number 1 signifying "liked a lot" and number five meaning "extreme dislike"—whether they liked or disliked each of the 37 programs. This paper-and-pencil test also asked respondents to identify the extent to which they considered themselves a "regular viewer of reality television." For purposes of conceptualization, a regular viewer was defined as "one who watches the show every week, and/or records episodes to avoid missing weekly broadcasts."

Data was obtained on other television viewing preferences by asking respondents to indicate how regularly they watch programs like news magazines, talk shows, reality programs, daytime serials, and other offerings and to identify the gratifications obtained from watching reality television.

To better understand the cognitive responses made when exposed to media content, a content analysis of the thoughts generated while watching reality TV was conducted. The researcher coded any and all thoughts that contained expressions of, or alluded to, social comparisons that participants "appeared to have" made spontaneously.

Participants were told that they later would see a segment of reality TV and encouraged to view that segment as if they were watching the program at home. While viewing the segment, participants were asked to record all their thoughts, and were given ample space to do so.

Data show that, of all the responses made concerning reality programming, most expressed some type of comparison between themselves and the reality show's stars. We conducted a content analysis of the thoughts and responses provided by the participants and found that, for the most part, men and women, as well as regular viewers and nonviewers, did not differ in terms of how they responded to people on reality shows.

People like knowing that there are others who are going though the same life experiences that they are and often make the same mistakes.

We then compared mood ratings obtained prior to viewing the reality show with those from immediately following exposure to the program. Analysis clearly indicated that regular viewers and nonviewers alike experienced a significant mood enhancement after exposure to reality television.

Living Vicariously

We know that reality television can captivate millions of viewers at any given time on any given day. Research has begun to document how people engage in automatic, spontaneous social comparisons when confronted by certain media images, particularly those of reality TV. We also know that one major effect of exposure to reality television is to feel better about one's own life circumstances, abilities, and talents.

Reality TV also serves as a much-needed distraction from the ongoing parade of tragic world events. It allows viewers an outlet by watching others overcome hardships, escape danger, live in a rainforest, land a dream job, learn to survive in Corporate America, and yes, even find love.

Whether the aim is money, love, becoming a rock star, creative expression, or just a chance to be seen on TV, the effect on audiences is the same. People like knowing that there are others who are going through the same life experiences that they are and often make the same mistakes. Despite the shifting desires of society and the fickleness of television audiences, the human need to compare and relate has provided a market for this genre.

So, while viewers realize they are not *America's Next Top Model*, may not have a chance at becoming the next *American Idol*, or even an *All American Girl*, they do enjoy the fact that, through a vicarious social comparison process, they can fall in love, win $1,000,000, or get the office snitch fired.

Organizations to Contact

The editors have compiled the following list of organizations concerned with the issues debated in this book. The descriptions are derived from materials provided by the organizations. All have publications or information available for interested readers. The list was compiled on the date of publication of the present volume; the information provided here may change. Be aware that many organizations take several weeks or longer to respond to inquiries, so allow as much time as possible.

Academy of Television Arts & Sciences
5220 Lankershim Blvd., North Hollywood, CA   91601-3109
(818) 754-2800 • fax: (818) 761-2827
Web site: www.emmys.org

The academy represents a range of television professionals from network executives to hair stylists who vote on nominees and winners for the annual Emmy Awards and College TV Awards. It publishes *Emmy Magazine* and sponsors events, workshops, and screenings of movies and miniseries. Its Archive of American Television, which produces a journal called the *Vault*, contains over four hundred interviews with actors, news anchors, producers, and other figures in the television industry.

Adbusters Media Foundation
1234 W. Seventh Ave., Vancouver, BC   V6H 1B7
   Canada
(604) 736-9401 • fax: (604) 737-6021
e-mail: info@adbusters.org
Web site: www.adbusters.org

Adbusters is a network of artists, activists, writers, and other people who want to build a new social activist movement. The organization publishes *Adbusters* magazine, which explores the ways that commercialism destroys physical and cultural environments. Spoof ads and information on political action are available on its Web site.

Ad Council

261 Madison Ave., Eleventh Fl., New York, NY   10016-2303
(212) 922-1500 • fax: (212) 922-1676
e-mail: info@adcouncil.org
Web site: www.adcouncil.org

The Ad Council is a nonprofit organization that works with businesses, advertisers, the media, and other nonprofit groups to produce and distribute public service advertisements, many of which are televised. The council also conducts research in order to improve the effectiveness of its campaigns. Studies and descriptions of its campaigns, which range from V-chip awareness to obesity prevention, can be found on its Web site.

Cato Institute

1000 Massachusetts Ave. NW, Washington, DC   20001-5403
(202) 842-0200 • fax: (202) 842-3490
e-mail: cato@cato.org
Web site: www.cato.org

The institute is a nonpartisan public policy research foundation dedicated to limiting the role of government and protecting individual liberties. It publishes the quarterly magazine *Regulation* and the bimonthly *Cato Policy Report*.

The Caucus for Television Producers, Writers & Directors

PO Box 11236, Burbank, CA   91510-1236
(818) 843-7572 • fax: (818) 846-2159
e-mail: bonnyinc@aol.com
Web site: www.caucus.org

The caucus represents producers, writers, and directors of cable or network television who believe that the American public is deserving of excellence in television programming. The Caucus Television Bill of Rights is posted on its Web site in addition to news, opinions, a calendar of events, and a members-only bulletin board. The organization produces the *Journal of the Caucus.*

Center for a New American Dream
6930 Carroll Ave., Suite 900, Takoma Park, MD 20912
(301) 891-3683
e-mail: newdream@newdream.org
Web site: www.newdream.org

The Center for a New American Dream is an organization whose goal is to help Americans consume responsibly and thus protect the Earth's resources and improve the quality of life. Its Kids and Commercialism Campaign provides information on the effects of advertising on children. The center publishes booklets and a quarterly newsletter, *Enough.*

Center for Successful Parenting
PO Box 179, Indianapolis, IN 46240
(317) 581-5355 • fax: (317) 581-5399
e-mail: csp@onrampamerica.net
Web site: www.sosparents.org

Founded in 1998, the center was created to increase awareness of the negative effects of violent media on children and to encourage the public to help shield children from media violence. On its Web site, the center offers facts on televised violence, reports on the content of old and new movies, and numerous articles, including "Can Violent Media Affect Reasoning and Logical Thinking?"

Commercial Alert
4110 SE Hawthorne Blvd. #123, Portland, OR 97214-5246
(503) 235-8012 • fax: (503) 235-5073
e-mail: info@commercialalert.org
Web site: www.commercialalert.org

Commercial Alert is a nonprofit organization whose goal is to prevent commercial culture from exploiting children and destroying family and community values. It works toward that goal by conducting campaigns against commercialism in classrooms and marketing to children. News and opportunities to take action against various marketing tactics are posted on the Web site.

Concerned Women for America (CWA)

1015 Fifteenth St. NW, Suite 1100, Washington, DC   20005
(202) 488-7000 • fax: (202) 488-0806
Web site: www.cwfa.org

Members of CWA work to strengthen the traditional family according to Judeo-Christian moral standards. The group supports the censorship of indecency and profanity on both broadcast and cable television. It publishes numerous brochures and policy papers as well as *Family Voice*, a monthly newsmagazine.

Federal Communications Commission (FCC)

1919 M St. NW, Washington, DC   20554
(888) call FCC (225-5322) • fax: 866-418-0232
e-mail: fccinfo@fcc.gov
Web site: www.fcc.gov

The FCC is an independent government agency responsible for regulating telecommunications. It develops and implements policy concerning interstate and international communications by television, satellite, cable, radio, and wire. The FCC also reviews the educational programming efforts of the networks. Its various reports, updates, and reviews can be accessed on its Web site.

MediaChannel.Org

575 Eighth Ave., New York, NY   10018
(212) 246-0202 • fax: (212) 246-2677
e-mail: info@mediachannel.org
Web site: www.mediachannel.org

MediaChannel.org, a nonprofit Web site, explores global media issues. In addition to news, commentaries, reports, and discussion forums, the site provides articles on children's advertising, TV news journalism, and public television. One of its news alerts is titled "Public Loses Twice: FCC Promotes Indecency, Then Censors It."

Media Coalition

139 Fulton St., Suite 302, New York, NY   10038
(212) 587-4025 • fax: (212) 587-2436
e-mail: mediacoalition@mediacoalition.org
Web site: www.mediacoalition.org

The Media Coalition defends the American public's right to access the broadest possible range of opinion and entertainment, including violent or sexually explicit material that is considered offensive or harmful. It opposes a government-mandated ratings system for television. On its Web site, the coalition provides legislative updates and reports, including *Shooting the Messenger: Why Censorship Won't Stop Violence.*

MediaWatch

PO Box 618, Santa Cruz, CA   95061-0618
831-423-6355
e-mail: info@mediawatch.com
Web site: www.mediawatch.com

MediaWatch challenges racism, sexism, and violence in the media through education and action. It does not believe in censorship but helps create more informed consumers of the mass media and a more active citizenry by distributing media literacy information. It makes available books, newsletters, and educational videos, such as *Don't Be a Television Victim.* On its Web site, MediaWatch provides current news and commentary on media issues, including the article "Murder, Sex, Mayhem: Tonight at Six."

Morality in Media (MIM)

475 Riverside Dr., Suite 239, New York, NY   10115
(212) 870-3222 • fax: (212) 870-2765
e-mail: mim@moralityinmedia.org
Web site: www.moralityinmedia.org

Established in 1962, MIM is a national, not-for-profit inter-faith organization that works to combat obscenity and to up-hold decency standards in the media. It maintains the National Obscenity Law Center, a clearinghouse of legal materials, and sponsors public information programs to involve concerned citizens. The *Morality in Media Newsletter* and the handbook *TV: The World's Greatest Mind-Bender* are published by MIM.

National Association of Broadcasters (NAB)

1771 N St. NW, Washington, DC   20036
(202) 429-5300- • fax: (202) 429-4199
e-mail: nab@nab.org
Web site: www.nab.org

NAB is a trade association representing the interests of radio and television broadcasters. It keeps its members abreast of technological developments, management trends, and research into matters related to the broadcasting of television, satellite, digital TV, and radio. Its Web site contains press releases, position statements, studies on audience viewing habits, legal testimonies, and information about public service campaigns. NAB's members receive weekly e-mail publications titled *RadioWeek* and *TV Today* as well as the monthly newsletters *Associate Monthly* and *NAB World*.

National Cable & Telecommunications Association (NCTA)

25 Massachusetts Ave., NW, Suite 100
Washington, DC   20001-1413
(202) 222-2300
e-mail: webmaster@ncta.com
Web site: www.ncta.com

Founded in 1952, the NCTA is the principal trade association of the cable television industry in the United States. NCTA's primary mission is to provide its members with a strong national presence and a unified voice on issues affecting the cable and telecommunications industry. Speeches, reports, and judicial filings can be accessed on its Web site. Members of the association also receive special reports and newsletters.

Parents Television Council (PTC)

707 Wilshire Blvd., Los Angeles, CA   90017
(800) 882-6868 • fax: (213) 629-9254
e-mail: editor@parentstv.org
Web site: www.parentstv.org

The goal of the PTC is to ensure that American television programming is values-driven. The PTC produces an annual *Family Guide to Prime Time Television* that profiles every sitcom and drama on the major television networks and provides information on subject matter that is inappropriate for children. On its Web site, the PTC posts movie reviews, television analysis: "Best & Worst of the Week," articles, and special reports. Its members receive the monthly newsletter, *PTC Insider.*

TV Turnoff Network (Formerly TV-Free America)

1601 Connecticut Ave. NW, Suite 303
Washington, DC   20009
(202) 518-5556 • fax: (202) 518-5560
e-mail: e-mail@tvturnoff.org
web site: www.tvturnoff.org

TV Turnoff Network is a national nonprofit organization that encourages Americans to reduce the amount of television they watch in order to promote stronger families and communities. It sponsors the annual National TV-Turnoff Week, when millions of Americans forego television for seven days, as well as a reading program called More Reading, Less TV. The organization prints the newsletter *The TV-Free American* three times a year.

Bibliography

Books

Mark Andrejevic   *Reality TV: The Work of Being
                    Watched*. New York: Rowman &
                    Littlefield, 2003.

Jack Benza   *So You Wannabe on Reality TV*. New
                    York: Allworth, 2005.

Jonathan Bignell   *Big Brother: Reality TV in the
                    Twenty-first Century*. New York: Pal-
                    grave Macmillan, 2006.

Anita Biressi and   *Reality TV: Realism and Revelation*.
Heather Nunn   London: Wallflower, 2005.

Sam Brenton and   *Shooting People: Adventures in Reality
Reuben Cohen   TV*. London: Verso, 2003.

Campaign   "Opinion: On the Campaign Couch
                    . . . with JB," August 10, 2007.

David S.   *How Real Is Reality TV? Essays on
Escoffery, ed.   Representation and Truth*. Jefferson,
                    NC: McFarland, 2006.

Dana Heller, ed.   *Makeover Television: Realities Remod-
                    elled*. London: Tauris, 2007.

Annette Hill   *Restyling Factual TV: News, Docu-
                    mentary and Reality Television*. New
                    York: Routledge, 2007.

Su Holmes and Deborah Jermyn, eds. | *Understanding Reality Television.* New York: Routledge, 2004.

Richard M. Huff | *Reality TV.* Westport, CT: Praeger, 2006.

Evan Marriott, John Saade, Joe Borgenicht, and Daniel Chen | *The Reality TV Handbook: An Insider's Guide; How To: Ace a Casting Interview, Form an Alliance, Swallow a Live Bug, and Capitalize on Your 15 Minutes of Fame.* Philadelphia: Quirk, 2004.

Susan Murray and Laurie Ouellette, eds. | *Reality TV: Remaking Television Culture.* New York: New York University Press, 2004.

Gareth Palmer | *Discipline and Liberty: Television and Governance.* Manchester, UK: Manchester University Press, 2003.

Matthew Robinson | *How to Get on Reality TV.* New York: Random House Reference, 2005.

Matthew J. Smith and Andrew F. Wood, eds. | *Survivor Lessons: Essays on Communication and Reality Television.* Jefferson, NC: McFarland, 2003.

Christopher J. Wright | *Tribal Warfare: Survivor and the Political Unconscious of Reality Television.* Lanham, MD: Lexington Books, 2006.

Periodicals

Glenn Baker

"From Boardroom to Boot Camp: Bill Rancic, the Inaugural Winning Entrepreneur on Donald Trump's Popular Reality TV Show, *The Apprentice*, Shares His Lessons on Life and Business Success," *NZ Business*, October 1, 2006.

Nora Caley

"Exporting 'Reality' TV to China: Denver's Red Robot Co-Produces Model Search," *ColoradoBiz*, February 1, 2007.

Lori Chordas

"Survival Skills: Life Lessons and Experiences Are Helping a TV-Reality-Show Winner Make the Transition from Firefighter to Employee-Benefits Salesman," *Best's Review*, July 1, 2007.

Eugene (OR) Register-Guard.

"He's No Fan of Reality TV; He's Just on It," December 29, 2006.

Roy G. Geronemus

"The Side Effects of TV Makeovers," *Skin & Allergy News*, December 1, 2003.

Elaine Misonzhnik Gotham

"Get in on the Reality Television Action," *Real Estate Weekly*, February 16, 2005.

Susan Gurevitz

"Reality Shows Push the Limits: Which Is Easier—Performing a Stunt on a Reality TV Show or Insuring the Show? Which Would You Rather Do—Eat Maggots to Win $100,000 or Insure a Reality TV Show?" *Risk & Insurance*, September 15, 2004.

Shirley Henderson	"From Reality Shows to Stardom: TV Showcased Their Talent and Changed Their Lives Forever," *Ebony*, November 2007.
Martin Hill	"The Real 'Reality' Behind Shock TV," *San Diego Business Journal*, October 28, 2002.
Irene Rosenberg Javors	"Reality TV: Escape from Reality?" *Annals of the American Psychotherapy Association*, March 22, 2004.
Marshall Lager	"Unreality Shows: They're Just a Way for Grown-Ups to Play Dress Up," *CRM Magazine*, October 2006.
Ron Leon	"Reality Television and Third-Person Perception," *Journal of Broadcasting & Electronic Media*, June 1, 2006.
Zizi Papacharissi	"An Exploratory Study of Reality Appeal: Uses and Gratifications of Reality TV Shows," *Journal of Broadcasting & Electronic Media*, June 1, 2007.
Linda Bates Parker	"'I Hate My Job': A Reality Check on Reality TV Shows," *Black Collegian*, February 1, 2005.
Robin T. Reid	"Political Reality TV," *Campaigns & Elections*, September 1, 2005.
Rem Rieder	"Surviving Reality Television," *American Journalism Review*, October 1, 2000.

Joel Russell | "Queasy Riders: Reality TV Shows Take Insurance Firms into Uncharted Waters," *Los Angeles Business Journal*, February 26, 2007.

Christopher Scanlon | "Christopher Scanlon on Reality TV," *Arena Magazine*, December 1, 2003.

Patrick Smith | "Inside Reality High (Teenagers Featured in 'American High' Reality-Based Television Program)," *New York Times Upfront*, May 14, 2001.

Brandon Voss | "Getting Stoned (Interview)," *Advocate*, January 30, 2007.

Louis Wittig | "God or the Girl? The Catholic Church Does Reality TV," *Weekly Standard*, April 13, 2006.

Index